THE HOLY FUCKS OF LIFE

CHANTEL ROSE

FriesenPress

One Printers Way
Altona, MB R0G 0B0
Canada

www.friesenpress.com

Pain is inevitable as we journey through this thing called life BUT don't allow your pain to manifest into a place of constant suffering. Think of your pain as a means to grow and amplify yourself to higher levels. Learn to ride the wave of pain into empowerment and bring forth bursts of unique creative expressions. So that you may fill the world with more passion and light for those souls lost in the dark. So those souls lost in the dark may be given a glimpse of their path back home. Stay true and remember your divinity. God bless.

ISBN
978-1-03-911276-6 (Hardcover)
978-1-03-911275-9 (Paperback)
978-1-03-911277-3 (eBook)

1. FAMILY & RELATIONSHIPS, ABUSE, DOMESTIC PARTNER ABUSE

Distributed to the trade by The Ingram Book Company

THE HOLY
F*CKS OF LIFE

*To all you f*cks out there: thank you for helping*
reveal the Holy Spirit within me.

CHANTEL ROSE

I dedicate this book to all children, meaning all of us!

By reading my book, I hope you can remember who you are:
God bless your soul, sweet child.

PREFACE:
EMOTIONAL TRIGGER WARNING

The Holy F*cks of Life wants to trigger you to remember everything in your life so you can pull up the suppressed memories you've hidden and expose them to the light for clarity. Do you know what memories I'm talking about? I'm talking about those haunting memories! The ones that come up and lead you into negative downward spirals, sending you into a depressive or anxious state of mind. The ones that trigger you to do bad things that you don't want to do and do things that may hurt yourself or others because those thoughts and memories are causing old wounds to resurface in very negative ways. I would like you to "exorcise" your demons, to give these memories and thoughts a good workout until they tire out and fall away from you, and as they fall away, you can pull your power back to you. I want you to send these memories and evil thoughts to the pits of Hell where they belong. I want you to think about cleaning out that negativity in the same way you would go to the gym to exercise your stress away. I want you to fight through your negative emotions and find your strength to pull them to the surface for cleansing to transmute from darkness to light.

The memories that started flooding to me in preparation for writing this book brought up all the old wounds, all the old feelings that I guess never truly healed nor had I let go of until now. I thought I had forgiven and thought through forgiveness brought healing, but maybe it only allowed me to have peace for a moment. The true healing came from honest reflection of how deeply affected I was in these dark moments. A genuine releasing of the negative energy within these wounds that no longer serve a purpose and can now be filled with love and light. As I started to reflect on my life, I began to remember many things, and it brought many tears and sadness but so much clarity. No matter how deeply moved I was by my memories, I allowed them to come through for clearing and cleaning of my soul. My hope, from this book, is that you may dive into your darkness and into the abyss, so you break the chains of all the painful memories you've buried yourself in, catapulting you to the surface so that you may rise above the deep waters of your emotions and into a new enlightened perspective. So you can move forward with a clearer conscience and a stronger passion and desire to live your best life with no destructive emotional chains where you will feel alive and free.

I had written the poems, which are at the beginning of each chapter, at specific critical points of my life. I felt I had no other way to express myself except through pen to paper, and as I wrote this book, I felt strongly guided to add passages from the bible to the end of each chapter. Again, all I ask while you read this book is to open your mind and sit with any emotions that might trigger you from my story. Sit with your feelings for as much time as you need and allow them to break through the surface so that you may cleanse that which no longer serves you, where you can find greater understanding in the world around you. I am asking you to remember. Can you remember your childhood? How far back can you go?

CHAPTER 1:
INNOCENT CHILD

Born into a world of lies, no one is right; we whisper to hide.
We stray into the shadows, knowing that's where tempters play.
Which means everyone's a victim, whether it's in night or day.
It attaches itself onto you until everything breath is spent.
It ticks away an unspoken clock, without vision but with resent.
Awareness holds a key:
So, what are we aware of if everything we see or seem is merely *a
dream within a dream?*
Survival is what we're taught, and love is rapidly becoming lost.
But love is what I live for without your approval or applause.

By: Chantel Rose

** The line *a dream within a dream* is from the famous Edgar Allan
Poe poem, "Dream within a Dream," published on March
31, 1849.

As a child, you are filled with wonder and wild excitement. The world
is full of unfulfilled potential and opportunities so vast that people lost
in the adult mind-frame laugh at what a child's mind can produce. Do
you remember? Do you remember your excitement with everything
anew? Do you remember coming into a world and the anticipation
that surrounded you felt so invigorating that it held space for unconditional love and acceptance of all? A world observed through a child's

eyes that had no judgments attached to it, just questionable wonder of what everything meant, the truth of it. Do you remember?

I remember. I remember it all too well. The good, the bad, the ugly, the lies, the abuse, the confusion, the pain, the suffering, the hopelessness, and the hypocrisy. I remember drowning in my childhood only to pull myself to the surface time and time again, the darkness trying to consume me consistently and making me physically ill. I remember fighting for my voice to be heard so that it wouldn't be lost in the ignorance of the adults around me who were supposed to know better, be better, and be able to lead by example. Instead, they were led blindly by their own state of disempowerment, addictions, fears, and anxious unknowns. I write this only from my childhood through my observations and by no means hold judgment on anyone, for judgment is reserved for only the one to give.

The depth of pain and empathy I felt over matters that I should not have known in my innocent years was not normal. I saw the pain in the faces of the adults around me, hidden behind their smiles because of unhealed childhood traumas looming over their heads, causing them to lash out in cruel ways toward the innocent—the ones they were supposed to love and protect. I could see glimpses into their pain and felt powerless in my efforts to draw attention to their truths because I didn't fully understand what I was seeing, but I know what it all meant then, now. Being able to read people from a mile away seemed like a curse and even more horrid when they knew I knew. The dark shadows that hide behind their eyes. The windows to the soul. The hollowed emptiness from their childlike innocence was stripped of them, and their divine spark was almost gone. Almost. Their darkness wanted to consume me along with them unconsciously because that was where their minds resided. Although my will was strong, my innocence and unconditional love allowed ill-intentioned people to come into my life who tried to strip me piece by piece until I was almost gone. Almost.

While they degraded, demeaned, abused, and betrayed me, I saw deeper into them than they could ever see for themselves. I saw the light in people and their potentials, but they became numb, just existing, dead and hollow inside because of the thick shadow that lay over their souls. Any light that pierced through that dark shadow, to shine on them, to heal them, seemed to burn them instead, and in the same breath, I was trying to heal them with truth, with light while they were trying to hurt me with lies and with darkness, but their projected pain and bitterness towards life slowly started to consume me as well. The hate the adults around me carried from past traumas and present circumstances was being cycled onto me. It was a cycle of abuse—generational curses—the pain that keeps going within families until someone breaks the vicious cycle. Any questions asked to find the truth was met with more fury. Any acting out or rebellion was met with abuse, but I was still full of love and hope. I still chose unconditional love for those who didn't know better, but I was so naïve in thinking they could change or choose differently. I just wanted their love and protection.

I remember one particular incident as a child. I was being whipped with a belt, and I had received so many that it just stopped hurting. I made the person hitting me aware that it had stopped hurting, and I stopped reacting to the pain. The strange thing is that I don't remember any more whippings after that incident once I stopped responding to the pain. Maybe it's because I started shutting it out, started becoming numb and disconnected, or perhaps because that form of discipline had stopped after that. Perhaps that reaction from me, the lack of response—the silence and surrender—made them aware that they were hitting a small child with a leather belt and made them question whether it was truly necessary to do. Are there no other ways to discipline and get your points across? I had asked myself *why*? What had I done to deserve that? What was the purpose of that? Why was that person so mad at me that they would hurt me like that? But I was just a kid and seemed to have been a bad one, apparently from the discipline I received, so what did I know.

Another incident I remember very clearly was when I had said some things that must've triggered deep emotions in someone as they aggressively charged towards me and their discipline turned into abuse. Grabbing me around my throat, they dragged me toward a flight of stairs as I was screaming for them to let go. They screamed profanities at me while I was trying to hold onto the stair railing, yet they ripped me off it. About halfway down the stairs, they then shove me the rest of the way down. I sat down there alone, in the dark, angry, crying, and confused. The person who did that to me would later come down and sit with me in the dark. I could feel that person was confused by how they had treated me and they started crying with me. They apologized and asked for my forgiveness, but all I could feel was resentment and anger. The only reply I could make out through my crying was simply *no*.

The memories I have as a child are haunting, but I can see now how they served their purpose and how those moments brought new awareness to my life. I would later have better skills for parenting, better ways of treating my children from all the unaware parenting I was afflicted with as a child. Though those were lessons I learned, I wished there had been more moments in my childhood when I truly felt loved and safe instead of a burden and a difficult child. Although I know I was difficult, I always stood my ground and still do.

My suffering as a child wasn't just emotional, and part of that was from being consumed by my thoughts of the brutalities of the world around me that I was acutely aware of, but it was also physical. It felt like I was always getting hurt by someone or something. I have scars all over my body that remind me of the pain I was constantly getting myself into as a child. One such incident was when I was on an adventure with another child from the same condo complex we lived in. We were in the back part of the complex, in a bushy forested area, and I just felt excruciating pain and let out a blood-curdling scream. I must've passed out from the pain because the next thing I remember was waking up wrapped in a blanket at a hospital. I don't know who was cradling me, but I remember my whole body burning and throbbing in pain; it felt so heavy just to hold my head up. Apparently, I had stepped on a hornet or wasp nest and got stung all over my little body. I was around eight or nine years old.

In another incident, around the same age, Grade 4, our gym teacher had just made me captain of the soccer team. I was able to choose my teammates and the name of my team, and I had decided on the Dream Team as our victorious name. After my team had won, a boy from the opposing team just came up and clocked me. Just right hooked me in the nose, and I dropped to the ground in pain. There was no reason for it from my perspective, but he was mad my team had won and he didn't like the excitement I was showing for winning. The teacher immediately grabbed him by his arm and brought him to the office. I remember feeling so defeated even though I had just won my first game with my Dream Team. Later in life, there would be many more moments when someone would come and try to rain on my parade in what could've been my happiest, most proud moments. Can anyone relate? Have these occurrences ever happened to you? Have you ever been attacked by someone for showing your happiness? Attacked for feeling happy and proud of yourself?

There is another incident, but further back in time. I was at my aunt's wedding rehearsal when I was around five or six, and I was the flower girl. I was in the church's basement playing with some other children and started running as fast as I could around one of the metal support poles when smack! I fell into that concrete so hard and learned that one of the other kids, a boy, stuck his foot out on purpose so I would trip. They laughed, thinking it was so funny. My mouth was in so much pain, and my dad picked me up and carried me out of the church. I remember my dad rolling up toilet paper and pressing it to my mouth and the stinging sensation just overwhelming me; I was screaming and crying, another hospital visit. I looked in the mirror and saw my lips triple in size from how swollen they had become and from the blood in my teeth. I still have a noticeable scar on my lip, a lump of scar tissue is a reminder for me, to this day, of the unnecessary cruelties done even amongst children for a good laugh. The noticeable scar stays for this lifetime on my face, which made me self-conscious for many years, but not anymore.

There were so many strange things I had endured as a child. My life seemed to be centred around painful moments, either from something I had done to myself or something someone else had done to me. When I reflect, it feels like my childhood was a constant cycle of pain. I was hospitalized numerous times as a child for stomach issues and pneumonia. Every year I seemed to get nasty respiratory illnesses. I was always sick, always on some medication or antibiotic. The banana flavour was my favourite flavour, amoxicillin. My stomach always seemed to bug me and had constant knots in it. It would feel like my insides were twisting in an excruciating way, and I couldn't eat because I would feel sick when I did.

I recall one hospital stay where I shared a room with a girl who was getting her tonsils out, and every couple of hours, I had blood drawn and was given medications that left me feeling so dizzy and out of it. I walked down the hospital hallway with my mom in such a daze as she heated some soup for me to eat. I remember the nurses; they were so patient with me. I was probably eight years old, and I especially liked the nurses on the night shift and would write them little notes saying how much I loved them for taking care of me. I would either slip the notes under my hospital room door or open my door a crack and throw them out onto the floor near their nurses' station. My grandmother would hold on to me and comfort me every time more blood work was needed, which meant more needles poked in me to take my blood. That hospital stay must've been a long one because I can clearly remember how the room was set up, and I still feel the emotions tied to that stay. My single bed with sterile metal rails was quite comfortable to sleep in, and all the teddy bears that surrounded me gave me comfort. I remember the cold floors when I walked to the washroom in my bare feet and just my hospital gown, with the soft, dim glow of the yellow light at night and the T.V room at the end of the hall that would let in so much natural light through during the day. I liked that room. I can't remember why I was there and what changed that I could leave the hospital. I don't remember going home healthy, and the problem was not resolved because I was sick for many years. I guess I just suffered from it—whatever it was—until I got older and started researching various healing methods, putting my health into my own hands.

Things seemed so different back then compared to now; as a mother myself, it seems surreal to even recall some moments because I would never wish any of the things I went through on my children. I have done everything in my power to consistently protect them, even when that requires me to take myself out of the equation for a moment because I have reached a breaking point, and I do not want them to be the victim of my pain. I choose to take a moment to step away from them to collect myself instead of taking a step toward them in aggression, frustration, and betrayal of their trust in me. So that I can be their guardian and be the guiding light for them, but like the imperfect humans that we are, I am a work in progress. I feel a parent should take themselves away and recollect themselves—go to the gym, have a bath, or just a night away to talk to someone about the difficulties that come with parenting. The time you take must have a purpose though; it can't just be time away to numb and ignore the challenges we face as parents. It must be a timeout to reflect on where your parenting is going wrong and come back wiser and with solutions. Parents need to come back into the equation knowing better and changing for the better. They must do this before they end up taking pieces of their children away because they haven't found how to put their pieces back together from their own unhealed childhood wounds.

I remember all those moments as a child that made me feel sick, sad, alone, in pain, and not taken care of in the way I wanted to be, but it made me become a wiser, more nurturing and loving parent. But, those moments in my childhood, many that I have yet to reveal, were also leading me into future abusive relationships because I had developed such a high tolerance for others' bullshit and projected pain, which helped create a darkness that grew within me. I was taught to brush all the pain and suffering under the carpet and was *told to stop feeling sorry for myself,* that *no one was listening to me cry,* and that I *should get over it already.* Such a cry baby I was, I suppose, but I hadn't lost my light yet. I hadn't felt hate yet, but the suffering started to lead me down a slippery slope. As a child, not knowing or understanding why people were so mean or how they could be so cruel to one another, or why they would do things to others just for the humour or the hell of it and justified it all, which eluded my innocent mind.

As a child, I could feel something transitioning inside me from all of that and it wouldn't be long before I had my first sip of alcohol at the tender age of ten, which was offered to many of us children that day by an adult. This person should've known better and should've been better, but ignorance is bliss, right? I clearly remember what kind of drink it was, a tube shot filled with electric blue liquor. The other children thought we were so cool and privileged to drink alcohol like the adults. The adult who gave us this shot had a cascade of darkness around him. I felt uncomfortable taking the drink from him but ignored the warning and drank it anyway. I could see the other children feel hesitant and unease as well, but we all wanted to be like the adults.

Like their states of drunken stupor, we wanted to think we were cool and out of control. We wanted to be noticed, and not just brushed aside as burdens. We wanted that unconditional love we were willing to give them without hesitation. Us children just wanted to feel safe, protected, and loved unconditionally, but adults always seemed to have conditions on us as to whether they treated us in a loving way or not. And so, we allowed ourselves to be led astray at that event. If we had listened to our inner guidance, we would've known that we didn't need to consume something to have fun. If we had an adult who noticed us for the children we were, we wouldn't have been led astray. As children, we were already in a state of silly, drunken stupor from our childish behaviours, so why were we drinking alcohol at that age? And why did that adult think nothing of it? Why were there so many times that adults thought nothing of it when it came to children? What happens in the transition between childhood and adulthood that makes adults forget their innocence, their inner child? I realized the love and attention that we, children, were always yearning for from adults couldn't be given to us because those adults could barely give love to themselves. They were seemingly lost. Those adults had already tuned out that inner child, so there was a separation between us. Our chaotic childlike innocence was frowned upon, and their will for us to grow up quickly was evident. They wanted to relate to us, and we wanted to relate to them. So began my descent into the dark.

> "Whoever receives one such child in my name receives me, but whoever causes one of these little ones who believe in me to sin, it would be better for him to have a great millstone fastened around his

neck and to be drowned in the depth of the sea. 'Woe to the world for temptations to sin! For it is necessary that temptations come, but woe to the one by whom the temptations come,'" Matthew 18:5-9 ESV

CHAPTER 2:
THE DIMMING LIGHT

A love so dear when you are so near, but what does it mean in
the end?
'Cause you fall in a trap and sometimes never come back, for you
have failed once again.
The love and the sorrow of sweet tomorrow, the past is behind
you now.
What shall you do than act like a fool as the past grows
farther away?
The past is regained; you now feel the pain:
The love and the sorrow of sweet tomorrow;
has the pain from the past to haunt you at last.
So, you now break down and cry, for the child's eyes are mine!

By: Chantel Rose

It's time to face any and all childhood trauma so that you can free
yourself of the negative emotional chains that bind you in your
current unhealthy attachments to people, places, and things that serve
no purpose to you anymore. Ask yourself, have you ever had that
entrenching feeling within, from a young age, that something was very
off in the world around you? Like it was upside down and backwards,
but everyone seemed fine with the growing problems surrounding
them? Did you feel homesick even when you were at "home"? As a
child and full of curiosity, did you ever notice that you stopped asking

questions around the pubescent stage, and your inner silence started to grow? Did you feel empty because of the awareness of yourself that was brought on by puberty? Did anyone tell you that your pubescent hormones were setting off your depressive and anxiety-driven episodes, or that you were an antisocial introvert, often hearing many state, "It's just a phase."? Was it just a phase? Can you relate? Was it at those points of dismissal that you hit a breaking point? When you were told that you didn't know anything, but in reality, you were just misunderstood. You stopped believing in yourself to answers the questions you were once so fervently seeking? Was it then that you bowed your head in defeat and stopped questioning authority because authority is always right, and you are always wrong?

Do you remember, as a child, when puberty hit? That a submissive type of autopilot kicked in, and you stopped expressing yourself? Did you stop wanting to be your unique self because it meant being different than your peers? Did you prefer to go with the grain than against the grain to avoid criticism? Instead, your only uniqueness came in hair colour, eye colour, skin colour, height, weight, and gender. All the physical aspects about your body that you can control and change to make you feel like you have a purpose and are exceptional while your inner being is silenced. Or when you can't control the chaotic storm brewing within you, and you feel the only control you have is on the physical and not mental level, do you harm your body? Could it be why some people want to jump out of their skin? Why some want to change their gender, cut themselves, delve into sex and drugs, or suffer from bulimia and anorexia, and the worst of all, suicide? Do you think it's because they feel like it's the only control they have while the world wants them to sit down, shut up, and do as others say, not as others do? Have you noticed the censorship of differing opinions that don't fit certain narratives? Teens like me who rebelled against standard societal thought patterns were ridiculed back in my days. We were shut down, and our voices were silenced before we could even state our opposing arguments. Do you remember the moments when your worth became less and less because your concerns fell on deaf ears like your feelings didn't matter?

***

I find it interesting how ignorant adults were and still are toward children. Life is short, and it was not that long ago that adults were once children; their little feet were running into the arms of those they loved for comfort and protection. What happens that makes adults forget that they, too, were once children? What happened that made the adults around me forget the innocence and the fragility of a child's heart, my heart? Nowadays, parents are so busy and caught up in the chaos around them that children are made to believe time and time again that they are burdens. Why are we so caught up in the world around us? Why is it so chaotic? Why are we so busy that we have forgotten what true peace feels like? That calm, sweet surrender. What happened that children are now too much and yet not enough all at the same time? Why do we have children sitting in classrooms for six hours a day, five days a week? Are we getting them prepared to become part of the working class of indoctrinated robots?

Children are tolerated instead of being given the effort and the time to be understood, guided, and nurtured properly. I feel like that comes from generational cycles repeating themselves that haven't been healed. We need to teach our kids how to properly discern what is best for them and what isn't instead of commanding them day in and day out: go to school, do your chores, do your homework, go to your sports, do this and do that. When we command, children have no time to sit and reflect on the world around them or come to conclusions on their own because they're being piled with information from outside sources. Yes, we want the best for them, but do you think filling their schedules is what's best for them? Do you think children can't have burnouts too? What do you think rebellion is? What do you think depression is? What do you think escapism with video games is or what outbursts are? I see adults having meltdowns every day, but the second a kid does that they aren't allowed to and are snapped at to behave appropriately! What about the adults? Many adults I see still haven't mastered how to calm the fuck down.

Is it no wonder that children nowadays drown themselves in electronics? Same with adults? They're escaping the real world for the fantasy world. Why are we always wanting to escape reality? When I reflect on my childhood, the children who needed that safe space to let their imaginations and unique creative gifts flow were instead being moulded into another one of those adults. The empty, anxious, angry, modern-day lost adult. I feel this happens because we were not able to understand our true essence when we were young. We knew it when we were young, but we had it almost beaten out of us and redirected to society's standard way of being. But I know that essence now. That essence never leaves us and sits within us, trying hard to come through to bring guidance and peace. Instead, people push it down and deny its existence and then wonder why they feel like they're drowning. Do you know that feeling? Panic attacks, anxiety, depression, and the internal chaotic storm getting out of control every so often. You have no clue what to do, so you ask the experts, thinking they will guide you better than your intuitive intelligence. Yes, they're there to help, but no one knows you better than you do. It's time to surrender and dive deep, for all the answers you seek are within you.

If we are honest with ourselves, most children, by the time they reach the teenager stage of life, are already systematically brainwashed to be a certain way. Children become conditioned into what society wants them to be, gearing them up to be society's perfect little specimen working bees. That system shoved all of us in the same box-type of agenda back then, and I see it for what it is now. The ones like me, who acted out against the norm or who couldn't handle being within that system, were medicated, counselled, demonized, and sometimes locked away. Do you think it's okay for people to be locked away for wanting a different way of being that isn't part of the system? I'm not talking about murderers, rapists, human traffickers, thieves, or criminals like that. I am talking about those locked away for asking, seeking, and exposing the truths of how twisted some indoctrinating systems are. Anyone seeking the facts seems to be looked at like a criminal just for wanting to know the truth or exposing it. #freeassange.

Although I was demonized and got into a lot of trouble for my aggressive truth-seeking ways as a teen, I was never given prescription medication or sent for counselling. Still, I know many children are put on all kinds of medicine to "correct" their behaviour. "Experts" will diagnosis a child with ADD, which turns into ADHD, leading to learning disabilities and bipolar disorder, along with having an overactive imagination and being a rebel without a just cause, or being an angst teen. After all of this propaganda is shoved in your face at such a young age, these so called experts, finally gets you snared in its trap. You stop. You obey. You follow blindly with no thought anymore, no questions, no critical thinking, just standardized ideals and a set of rules for you to abide by. Although it is what it is, is it right? What would you do with the truth if you knew it?

Society will use teens' rebellious nature and how "experts" corrected such behaviour with medication as an example for others, and others will follow blindly. They keep children, who think differently, in line—numb and docile or in fear—with the tactics they've created to get children to submit and obey their orders. These "different" teens then travel into the dark pits, alone and scared, not wanting any trouble to come their way. Those that think differently will start to hide their true identities and their authenticity in fear of being persecuted. Those who deny their truth, their authentic selves, start to grow scar tissue around the wound of despair—their hearts—until that internal pain and heaviness almost seem normal because they can't feel their heart beating anymore, emotionally numb and emotionally unavailable. Or maybe they've been medicated through big pharma's pill-popping prescription plans. You know the plans I'm talking about, don't you? The plans that keep you medicated until you die or until what is abnormal feels normal. There are never any cures, only one prescription after the other until the lies they feed you become your truths. Robots. Stand in line. Swallow. Next. Repeat.

Do you think the types of people that have formed the societal constructs and extreme religious doctrines that we see in the world today know the damage they're doing? Do you know who I speak of? Those who oppress people and strip children of their innocence and try to take away a child's light, so when they move into adulthood they won't reach their full potential? The tyrants of the world who feel the need to control others. Do these types of controlling, narcissistic entities not know the consequences that will follow their oppressions of people and suppressions of truth? Do they not know the pain that they put on others? Do they know that their selfish greed will come for them at a high price in a much different form, one they aren't accustomed to? Do they not know that justice, though it may not come swiftly, comes nonetheless in its divine timing? They must not know their times of lying, oppression, indoctrination, and suppressing truths are over, but it is time someone told them.

Also, when it comes to the indoctrinating school system and before you start to think I am against systematic schooling, I am not, for the most part anyway. I value the way of a teacher as they are the ones who want to educate and give children their best shot moving into the working-class system. I want to shout out to all the teachers who are doing their best but struggling in a failing system. A system for a one-size–fits-all scenario that doesn't work for everyone except those that can handle the schooling systems boxed in ways. Even then, how are those children handling it? I know teachers want what's best for the children, but how can teaching every person the same thing, the same way, work? Is that why there is a rise in learning disabilities? I think school is suitable for creating a form of discipline and focus because it makes you have to sit and concentrate on specifics topics, but at what point are the specifics supposed to be for a one size fits all type of scenario. Like I said, and we all know, not everyone is the same. Not everyone thinks the same. Not everyone has attention spans that can last as strongly as another. Not all children are born to be equal or to understand the same concepts in the same way, yet we push the same systematic agenda for all. No wonder children are more medicated now than ever. Children are kept docile enough to stick to the program that is forced on them, but not enough where they're complete robots, yet. You'd be surprised how many people don't want you thinking for yourself; they do't want you to have too big of dreams because it'll make them feel smaller. People like that will tell you, *It's too big of a risk, It won't work, You'll fail,* and *It's too out of reach.* The outside voices just keep sabotaging you and your dreams. Eventually, you become your worst critic, and those static external voices don't help.

When do we start figuring out and focusing on specific natural gifts of each child so that they may reach their full potential in this lifetime? So that they may become the masters of something specific to them. Why do people wait so long? Wait until the weight of the lies gets so heavy that it forms itself into a mid-life crisis', mental breakdowns, depression, and worst of all, suicide? It's rare that people overcome the issues that cause them so much stress and can say to themselves that they've had enough of the bullshit. Instead, they find it easier to medicate themselves with alcohol, drugs, sex, and anything to avoid searching for the answers they so desperately seek. If only we could all rise above and find what's true for us, the truth of all things. It's rare that people will seek their truth, their natural ability to prosper, and it's sad to know that people would choose to stay stuck in repetitive toxic cycles because it seems easier. People choose to follow the robotic protocols and ways of living in our seemingly free world but it's really a world full of indoctrinating systems. Why do they try to throw us all in a box filled with the same ideas and same concepts, over and over, expecting a more successful result, only to see its failure. Only to see a rise in all kinds of learning disabilities and a rise in mental health issues. Think about it, what's the definition of insanity? Look up the definition. Do you see the world around you with an honest, open perspective? **#savethechildren**

......

Now ask yourself, do you feel free enough to express yourself authentically? And if you express yourself authentically, would it be for the good of humanity? Do you know your truth, the whole truth and nothing but the truth? Or has society created a monster in you from its lies? Who. Are. You?

......

I hope I didn't lose you by having you dive deep into those questions. If you need a moment to push pause and sit with these words, please do. Downloading and absorbing information is a process. A process you should take delicately. I would like us to go back to that nagging feeling I mentioned at the beginning of this chapter. How everything just didn't feel as it should and that the world seemed off. That nagging feeling led me down a path of self-teaching, of self-seeking, and of self-soothing ways to cope with the upside-down and backwards world around me. I fell in love with reading books, and then I fell in love with writing. I could read anything with an open mind, but if the content felt off or I didn't resonate with it, I would move on quickly. I needed to feel the value I would gain from where my time was being invested. I needed to focus on things that would genuinely teach me something helpful instead of leaving me feeling bored, unfocused, and stuck in a repetitive cycle.

I needed concepts that I could absorb, concepts that felt true to me, and concepts that I could understand on a deeper level. I didn't want to read something just to memorize it so I could pass a test. I needed ideas that weren't pushed on me aggressively, as I already felt this push to believeideals that I didn't align with. So, it's no surprise that when it came to reading books within the context of school, I could hardly pay attention and barely got by. My rebellious nature was starting to grow in those teen years, and my teachers knew how I felt. I had strong opinions from the beliefs I was forming, in opposition to the world around me, and at such a young age. I was not a child who agreed with the system in place or with what I saw in the world around me. It dulled me, and it was difficult for me to handle.

The school system and I were barely getting by, and some teachers, who remember me, might say I was an average student. I actually enjoyed school until Grade 5, and as I had mentioned earlier, something changed when that puberty stage hit. Maybe it was just a phase, or perhaps it was my awakening even more from a slumber. Perhaps I was becoming more aware of the faulty system and the corruption of the world around me. I rapidly started disconnecting from that system; it didn't seem to fit how I felt I should be learning. I felt school was trying to take something from me rather than give me an education. I was getting in trouble, skipping school; I had already started drinking, smoking cigarettes and weed by the age of thirteen. I can see how the adults around me attributed my rebellious nature to my substance use, and maybe it was, but they knew what I was doing, and no one stopped me from doing it. No- one stopped me from sneaking booze, no one stopped me from getting cigarettes, and no one stopped me from stealing my older sister's weed. We were all just having one hell of a time avoiding everything, and no one bothered to tell me that I was leading myself down a destructive path.

I changed schools three times between junior high and high school. In one school, I called a teacher out on his inappropriate behaviour and sexual harassment toward his students, specifically the inappropriate sexual comments he made to me. I went to the principal's office to see what could be done about this, only to be told that I was a liar and had to leave that school. How nice of them to make me feel like that, a child, a child who was apparently a liar, who knows nothing, and was always wrong, right!? We wonder why children, and females in particular, are so silent about the injustices done to them. I know there are people in this world who lie about serious things like that, but I am not one of them. The most interesting thing about that situation was years later, he was exposed for who he was. Funny how the truth revealed itself in its own time, and justice did end up being served with no added effort of my own.

If being sexually harassed by a teacher wasn't enough, how about I put myself in a school with a bunch of viperous groups just waiting to attack at any chance they got. The clicky groups who had nothing better to do than treat anyone else like shit. I would walk down the hallway wearing a baggy pair of jeans and my dad's t-shirt, and they would start calling me slut, skinny bitch, bulimic, and pizza face (I had terrible acne). I had no style what's so ever, I was weird, and I definitely didn't think like that group of mindless people, so of course, I was a target. One group of bullies, the summer bullies I called them, would follow me home from school and to the swimming pool and threaten to beat me up. I would mind my own business, just trying to do kid things, and these girls just wanted a fight out of me, always trying to provoke a response out of me. They even showed up at my house a few times to threaten me.

My summer bullies, were the worst they didn't go to the same school as me but they did live in my hometown and had nothing better to do than to cause trouble. They harassed and bullied the people around them with no consequences, or so it seemed. The bullying was so bad that at one point, my parents called the cops on that group for constantly stalking and harassing me, but that didn't seem to help. Those teens picked me apart every chance they got. I eventually started to stick up for myself; I was terrified of doing that, but I realized that I had to do something because nothing else was working. No amount of police phone calls or parental meetings seemed to stop the bullying, so it was my turn to try. It was surprising how much power I had in threatening those that threatened me.

The sad thing about this story is that some of those bullies, it was later discovered, had very deep-rooted issues that they were going through at the time. They had been projecting their pain onto me and to those around them. Again, their childhood innocence was stripped from them, and their voices fell on adults' deaf ears. Who was there to listen? Who was there to save them? Who was there to lean on? Who was there to provide comfort? It seemed these bullies found it much easier to project their pain than to feel it. It was easier for them to pretend they weren't hurting inside, and they found it easier to inflict hurt on those around them than face the truth of the pain in their lives. The other bullies who really went after me, with so much intent to inflict pain and frustration on me, would later have tragic things befall on their families. I wonder if it was worth it to treat people the way they did, to get away with so much pain? They even treated their family members the same, and that caused such a horrific travesty amongst them. I wonder if they have remorse.

I find it interesting to reflect on how bullying was becoming a growing theme in my life; the projection of others' pain onto me. The truth was revealed after the damage was done. I seemed to be an enemy to so many people who did not have a just cause to treat me the immoral way they did, but I know I wasn't the only one going through this. I remember hearing about a group of kids around the same age (thirteen) who were also being bullied. They were going through their own terrible times, but they weren't the type to take their problems out on others. I had caught wind of a disturbing pact these kids made—since these teens were suffering and they didn't know what else to do—and they decided to kill themselves together at the same time! They wanted to die together! They had gotten to the point where they did not want to live anymore. I think there were around six of them. This group of friends had written their notes, and they were ready to go, but an intervention occurred when. I spoke up and told my mom what I knew about this situation. My mom notified the school and the school notificed these childrens parents and this suicide pact was stopped, but the underlying issues weighing these teens down to the point of suicide weren't dealt with. Their emotional pains weren't resolved, but pills for pain could suppress it all. So, prescribe away doctors and throw a pill in their mouths, hoping that their internal oozing wounds won't reach the surface anymore. Just let it fester inside; as long as it doesn't show its ugly face on the outside anymore, all will be well. Right parents? Right doctor?

I mean really, have you noticed the rise in anxiety, depression, suicide, and the use of prescription pills like it "ain't no thang" but the latest trend? Have you noticed anyone pop an anti-anxiety drug with a glass of wine as the new go-to way to fill the void? Those empty, doe-eyed, valium/Percocet soccer moms with little to no emotion? Where there's a problem, there's a prescription. Right? We live in a seemingly more convenient and useful environment, so what's the problem? We have more ways of entertaining ourselves to keep us happy and more distracted than ever before. So, what's the problem? Why all the pre-scriptions, why all the suppression, why all the pain within the people of this world? Do you see what's normalized these days? That shouldn't be! Do you know what keeps you from the truth?

My rage at the world, and its wrongdoings on us children, was really starting to grow at that point, and my words would soon begin to cut like a knife to those who would not listen. I was becoming very argumentative. I was in constant battles in school—with people in general—either defending myself, rebelling against everything, or helping kids who were bullied. As I created problems for myself, I felt like I could solve everyone else's problems. Make it make sense! One interesting thing I noticed about helping bullied kids and adults to this day was that when I intervened to help the victim, sometimes the victim ended up turning against me. Suddenly, I became the target. Has this happened to you? Holy fuck that was a hard lesson to learn. It is infuriating to see how many people have no integrity and how many cower under pressure. Those people who were being degraded, demeaned, or abused knew what was happening to them was wrong, and they knew those people were not good. Yet, the second they had a chance to get up with the help of my hand, they saw an opportunity to pull me down! The people I would try to help ended up throwing me to the wolves. Instead of them running away to escape, they saw that I was now the target and would join the wolves for the attack, just for the hell of it! Why are people like that? People are all sorts of upside down and backwards, and nothing seems to change. Is this a society made of vultures?

It's an intoxicating thing to dehumanize someone else. I saw the momentary power in these people's eyes from belittling, degrading, and demeaning another human being. The sneer that crept across their faces and the sick laughter that would follow. Thinking that humiliating another human being was just the funniest thing ever. I could see the empty power pulsing through them, giving them that short-lived satisfaction. I could see the pain being shifted from these darkened souls onto someone else, and for a moment, this projection became peace for that hurting, abusive human. I've always been deeply disturbed by the things I can see, the things I can feel, and the pain people hide. I know people do horrible things to themselves and to others to justify the loss of power they feel within themselves. I do not know who is taking their power, confidence, or love away from them, but I see them stripped and bare, and I can sense their pain behind the projection. That's why I've always been able to forgive because most people do not start off as monsters. Monsters are created as a product of their environments. Most people become monsters because they couldn't or didn't know how to master the pain and transmute it into something else, something more beautiful, something that could help heal humanity.

Through enduring painful situations and feeling the power that comes from forgiveness, I've also come to realize that I must be careful because with forgiveness comes a high tolerance for bullshit and shitty people. If you can endure a lot of pain and suffering from people and still forgive quite quickly, you need to protect yourself and learn to let go of these people before it's too late. Forgiveness does not mean you should stick around to be used or constantly drained of your good nature to the point of burnout, breakdowns, or illness. The monsters within people see that forgiving nature from a mile away, and they can suck you dry of your energy if you aren't careful. If you don't create healthy boundaries with these types of people or anyone for that matter, they can and will start using you as their doormat, as their own personal slave. They are energy vampires and narcissists. You will become their drug dealer for their next fix as they become addicted to your essence, to your goodness, to taking your power away and feeding it to their monster within. They'll dump their weight on you because they know you are a forgiving and a strong person, and they won't think twice about how their added weight could suffocate you. If the weight is off their backs, and there's more life to suck from you, that's all that matters to them.

I hope I have painted enough of a visual to show you how these young years were not enjoyable but brought me more awareness. As an adult, I can see now how aware I was back then, through my questioning of everything. As far back as nine years old, I can recall the start of dark periods in my life. I believe darkness has its purpose. Even though I was a child holding so much love and forgiveness in my heart, it all felt so heavy, as it should've, because other people's pain was wearing me down. I had also started questioning religion within that period of my life. I started asking why people went to church to worship God when we can worship him no matter where we were. I started saying that Catholicism was the first form of government and did no service to humanity other than to enslave it. Yes, I did believe that. I still don't really know how I came to that conclusion at a young age. I questioned it all, and my family didn't even go to church. I would ask why people had to go to church to be forgiven, and why go to church to get into heaven? I would ask and ask and find no answers, but I asked the wrong people. I asked people who did not have a strong belief system or strong faith in anything, including themselves. I asked people who were going by society's whims, society's schemes, people who were being blindly led by implanted impulses from the toxic environment that surrounded them. When I was about fourteen, I had started to clean up my act and my ways when I started looking into God and the ways of Jesus; when I started looking for the truth. There was no more drinking, no more weed, and I had started walking a straighter and narrower path. I searched for ways to be better, feel better, and I began searching for some concrete truths.

I needed answers, but who was there to answer these kinds of complex questions? When I hit that puberty hormonal stage, and I was blindly walking into the teenage stage of life, I needed all sorts of questions answered. I had no idea what the fuck was going on; we didn't have Google back then! I had an older sister, but her distaste for me was evident by how she treated me, so I didn't bother to ask her for much. My parents, well, although they were there, they weren't really there like I needed them to be, but that's how most teens think about their parents, isn't it. All of these questions led me on a search of my own, spending hours in libraries, reading through all sorts of different religious books, and then tapping into various other subjects to expand my thinking and perspective. I was trying to find some kind of guidance and peace of mind through those insecure and anxiety-driven teenage years.

I felt way too deeply and thought way too deeply at that age about many things. The insecurities that come with being a teenager hit you at once, no matter how good a life you have or how much knowledge you've been given about that stage of life. I mean, just the changes the body makes are overwhelming in itself. You have acne galore, and your body changes in ways no one told you about. You start to stink. Your sex drive starts to get out of control because of all the hormones flooding your system, and you don't even understand what that is, but you can feel it. Although there was a sex education VHS tape describing all these changes back in Grade 4, I don't remember learning anything from it. We laughed so hard with the teachers at the seemingly strange and inappropriate content on that video. I distinctly remember my teacher just howling and was so red-faced. It was such an awkward and we probably shouldn't be watching this in Grade 4 uncomfortable kind of laugh. Yet, it was nonetheless a deep, belly laughing, hysterical moment for everyone in homeroom that day.

Anyway, as if that puberty body transition wasn't hard enough to go through, I wanted to make life even harder, apparently. Yet again, I had decided to switch schools, trying to escape all the chaos and pain that just kept trying to swarm me. Though at that point, a window of opportunity had come knocking on my door. I had a chance to escape my small town. A chance to run away from the pain and suffering I felt I was going through. I had an opportunity to be free!.

I had just come home from playing in a hockey tournament, and my dad and older sister had just got home from some modelling competition. My dad was hyping me up about how I would do so well in it, and I should go try out and go with them the next day. I was a major tomboy with no style and so awkward, so I hemmed and hawed about going, but he and my sister finally convinced me to go, and so I went. When we arrived at the modelling competition, around five hundred girls were there from all over the area. I ended up placing in the top five. So, there I was, signing my first contract with a local modelling agency and was being told I had a promising modelling career. Woohoo! Where I once had no direction and had been full of teenage angst, I then had a golden opportunity to become something more than all the bullshit I was surrounded by. After feeling confused and alone for so long, it felt amazing to have this exciting turn of events happen in my life. I felt hope. With this opportunity, my life seemed to be getting so much brighter, and it did for a time, but it wouldn't be long for me to realize it was creating space for something darker to enter.

"The light shines in the darkness, and the darkness has not overcome it." John 1:5 ESV

CHAPTER 3:
TRUTH OR LIES

Truth. Lies. Truth. Lies. TRUTH LIES!?
I don't know . . . does it lie? Is it lies?
What do you gain from knowing? Knowing love . . . knowing life .
. .
Siphoned away in a crippled memory of what was thought to
havebeen true
that maybe wasn't . . . lies.
Or is it and will always be a pain in your soul . . . from truth . . .
from lies.
That maybe exists and fills your life form with knowledgeable
dedication to be.
A REASON TO EXIST!?
Blindly walking, blindly feeling, blindly being . . .
WHAT!? Truth . . . OR . . . lies.
Such frustration of not knowing, but what comfort being told you'll
never know.
Life is a mystery . . . BUT IS IT!?
Anything born will be dead. Anything dead will be reborn?
Anything created can or will be destroyed?
Children . . . the only truth. Children . . . the only things
still whole...eee.
Children . . . are the only ones that know and understand.
UNTIL
They beome corrupted. They become lost. They become used.
They become manipulated. They become US!

Children become eaten alive by everything created, everything
destroyed, everything done!
Children are fed to society's impulses, washed away in TRUTH
from LIES!
In truth . . . lies sick, weak despair!

By: Chantel Rose

In the early 2000s, what the ideal teenage girl should look like and
how they should act was greatly distorted, and my insecurities were
at an all-time high with the added pressure of becoming a model. I
never considered myself pretty or model material. I thought of myself
as an ugly duckling because my family members told me I was. The
Chinese-looking ugly duckling; one of my friends had even called me a
mutt because of my mixed ancestry. A *Heinz 57*, they said. Although I
am not Chinese, I am of mixed origin, Métis. My diverse look caught
the eye of modelling agents; they thought I looked exotic. I am athleti-
cally built, muscular, healthy-looking, but as a teen, I had bad acne,
and I was tall for my age, 5'8 at fourteen years old. I towered over my
friends; I was just long and gangly and had always felt awkward and
weird because of my body. I also felt like an outcast because of how my
thought process worked; it differed from others. Maybe I felt like an
outcast and had these negative feelings about myself because of who I
surrounded myself with and my environment.

My environment was full of jealous people who heard of my opportunity. With the negativity from others, I also became quite aware of
how I should look to the public eye, and it became overwhelming at
times because I had to uphold a particular image. There were just so
many ads everywhere promoting unhealthy body images and unrealis-
tic expectations, along with exploitations of young girls. Fourteen-year-
old super models displayed across the cover of magazines in Calvin
Klein underwear and sometimes topless with their little fourteen-year-
old girl arms draped across their flat, undeveloped chests! This was/is
normal!? **#cancelporn**

With the constant bombardment of advertisements, movies, and magazines, I felt like I had to eat a certain way, dress a certain way, and act a certain way. Teen heartthrob movies, back then, had girls acting ditzy, slutty, or bitchy, all for the attention of the oh-so-good-looking jockstraps! The popular boys—jockstraps—, also seemed to be the ass-holes in the movies. Girls were told to change their entire persona to gain the acceptance of assholes and the popular crowd's approval, and most of the time those assholes didn't even care about the girl because it was all a façade. What a time to be alive; that's what teenage life felt like back then, fake and filled with drama, drama, drama. But now that I think about it that shit carried over into adulthood and if you think about it a little more, we all seem to be led by the latest trend, the latest gossip, and the latest product. Televisions seem to act like a programmer that directs you straight toward something you probably shouldn't want or have in your life, but on impulse, you do what the TV tells you to do anyway. Watching TV is meant for entertainment purposes only, right? I mean television, Tell-A-Vision and an array of "programs" to choose from, then you sit down ready to CHANNEL into that PROGRAM, and the show CASTS thoughts and ideas into your brain, consciously and subconsciously, whether you're aware of it or not. Use search engine *Duck Duck Go* and search "Operation Mockingbird!" Are we modern-day slaves being programmed? Are we being led blindly to our own doom?

......

Just a few words of advice, if you don't want to be programmed a certain way, shut off your TV and stop being sucked into propaganda that can make you make the wrong decisions out of fear. Stop being driven by the advertisements that surround you that drive you to become impulsive. Carve your own path, put your feelers out and let your spirit guide you. Learn to discern between the truth and lies and the good and the bad. Be good. Do good. Feel good. I know, I know, easier said than done.

......

29

When you think about it, the ideals back then are nothing like today because today you are not allowed to body shame. It was ok back then for a modelling agent to look at me, skin and bones, and tell me I was too fat and that I needed to lose more weight if I was going to land a modelling gig. I can't tell you how many times I was told that, along with many other young people in that industry. You can only imagine the road this led me down; I stopped eating, for the most part, consuming one meal a day. I started taking sleeping pills to try and sleep away the hunger pains. No one noticed, and no one asked. I can see how children slip through the cracks because "grown-ups" are in their own world of pain, of sin. I noticed the adults around me could barely handle their own shit, let alone find solutions to their problems, so that's how children slip through the cracks. I mean, how would they be able to solve any of my problems when so many of their problems went unsolved. I felt like I was walking a lonely road and I was!

The road may have been lonely, but it wasn't for nothing, and all those hunger pains had finally paid off. This small-town girl just won 1st place in a big city modelling competition. I was on the news and got to be in a commercial for the local modelling agency. I was over the moon! Best of all, that first-place prize was sending me to beautiful Vancouver to compete in an international modelling competition with other fresh-faced children from all over Canada. I remember that trip so well, the ocean breeze, the tall glass buildings surrounding me, all the lights. It was nothing I had seen before because I had come from such a small town. The closest city I had been too had nothing on the beautiful city of Vancouver. It was full of such diversity, so much life and such good energy that it was invigorating for me.

Going to Vancouver for that modelling competition is one of my favourite moments that I've captured in my memories. A hope-filled moment for a better future that was filled with excitement at the potential for a better life. The essence of that memory, of my child-like yonder, refreshes me every time I think about it. The new feelings that sparked within me and brought forth such a different type of energy and emotional response to the world around me. It became more beautiful somehow. I felt renewed, and from that renewed feeling, I was ready to ditch my small town and go out into the world of fashion to make a name for myself. But first, I had to land a more significant contract. I had to land a contract that brought my face to the international modelling side of things.

It wasn't long after that trip to Vancouver that I landed an international modelling contract with one of the most sought-after modelling agencies of that time, Ford Models. From that competition in Vancouver, I was told I'd be making my way to Toronto, so I went back home to pack up again. It was the first time for my mom and me to go to Toronto. My mom and I stayed at the model house to get accustomed to where I would be living once my mom left. While we were there, I did a few photoshoots for my portfolio and got to know the people who worked at the agency. It felt surreal. Such big things were happening for this small-town girl who was still only in high school.

The model house I was going to be living in was beautiful. The woman who owned the house also lived there and was a model and a close friend of my agent. She made me feel so welcome and taken care of, and we were shown the inner city and got to guest spot on a couple of shows that aired live downtown. One network that we were invited to, which was my favourite, was Much Music's on-air live show, Electric Circus. Music networks used to be awesome, especially Much Music and their VJ's back then. I thought I was living in a dream with all the neat things that were happening around me on that first trip. When it was time to leave, my mom and I flew back home, and I started preparing to move to Toronto by myself. My dad bought me my first cell phone in preparation for my solo journey. It was a cute little silver Samsung flip phone, I think. Regardless, I was to the moon and back from all the little details that were filling themselves in for what was soon to come. I was eating healthy, working out, drinking green tea regularly, had my mind straight and was so focused, just doing what I could to be healthy. I was mentally preparing myself to go, and before I knew it, it really was time to go back to Toronto!

My suitcases were packed, and we were driving to the airport. I vaguely remember the drive, but I remember it was winter because it was cold, and the ground still had snow on it. I also remember getting to the airport and being told I was on a red-eye flight. I had no idea what that meant until I was boarding the plane at midnight and thought, *Ahh, I get it now.* I was flying with Air Canada, and I remember I had these pink pyjamas on because I was planning on sleeping through that five-hour flight. I had the teddy bear that I had been given when I was born, and I had decided to take on my journey; after all, I was still just a child, right? Oh, those last moments in the airport waving my family goodbye were surreal. My curly hair was just a mess, and I didn't have a fucking clue what I was doing. I was nervous and scared, but away I went. Here I come, Toronto, time to forget the rest. I did end up sleeping that whole flight, and when I landed in Toronto, I waited patiently for my suitcases and then flagged a cab. I had a notebook filled with the addresses I needed, and I hopped into that cab with slight fear but a lot of excitement. I got to the model house around 8:00 am and was greeted by the same lovely woman I met before who would be my host for the months to come.

The first day I got settled in and unpacked because I had to figure out my way around the city the next day. I walked by Queen Street and Bathurst with all the scaffolding over the sidewalks and was scared to walk underneath it in fear of it falling on me. I would walk past Much Music and all the other big broadcasting stations with my headphones on, listening to my Discman, feeling almost like I was on another planet because it seemed so surreal. My modelling agency was on Spadina Ave and Queen Street, and that area had these beautiful old brick buildings. There were boutique spas, and restaurants within these buildings tucked away in these unique spots. Though they looked somewhat ruined on the outside, it was a completely different story on the inside. Although I had enjoyed discovering the city by myself, I was happy to reconnect with the friends I had made on my first trip to the city, and they showed me all the gems of Toronto.

Although this enchantment was happening around me, the potential to suck me into the party scene was there, but I was walking a very straight and narrow road at the tender age of sixteen. I mean I was busy, I had to keep up with my schooling through modules, make sure I got myself to all my casting calls, learn the transit system to make my way around the city, and keep up with my workout routine and healthy eating plans! So, that all took up the majority of my time. Life was going smoothly; I stayed out of trouble and kept to myself for the most part until I was moved into the bottom level of the model house. You see, I had been living in the attic portion of the house, all the way at the top level. The model house was actually a huge townhouse, just off Queen and Crawford, with several floors. I was at the top; the owner was on the floor beneath me, along with two other bedrooms and a bathroom, then the kitchen and living areas below that floor, and then there was the basement. The basement housed the other models who were all older than me, and that was where my troubles began again.

There were four of us living in that basement level. The basement suite had a lovely little kitchen and fair-sized living room, as well as a tiny area outside the bathroom to do your make-up. The bathroom was weird, though, because it was tiled everywhere, but the shower. There was no separation between the shower and other portions of the bathroom, and there was no shower curtain. It was the first time I had seen a bathroom like that, so I thought it was strange, and I didn't like it. Other than that one dislike, the basement suite was quite cute and accommodating. I had my own room with a small cable TV, and it felt super cozy. Right beside my room was another girl's room that was about the same size as mine, and then, past the common areas, there was an oversized room that two other models shared.

All of us girls had become more like sisters than mere roommates, and we always tried to look out for each other. We started going to castings together and started attending model events together. Pretty soon, we started hitting the party scene together. You can see how this was beginning to turn me away from the straight and narrow path I was trying to hold on to. I had a gang of hot girl models to go out with and lead me into the clubs. We would get so much attention any time we went anywhere, and that's where it started getting wild for me; it just started to get out of control. No one really questioned my age, but if they did, I lied, and no one pressed the question further. I skipped lines at the hottest clubs and got VIP service as soon as I walked in.

I never ever opened my wallet, and I don't even know if I carried one around at that time because I never needed it. I never even thought about needing an ID because it was rare anyone asked for it and if they did I always told them I was of age and that was always enough back then. I met many people in that nightlife scene and had started partying with in interesting group of people. I knew I was becoming well known in the club scene when I would just walk up to security and know them by name and give them a hug as I walked into the VIP area. Surreal. I was still just a kid, but me, oh my, oh my, oh me! The stories I have, the parties I went to, the secrets I heard, and this was just the start of my trip!

> "Even though I walk through the valley of the shadow of death, I will fear no evil, for you are with me." Psalm 23:4

CHAPTER 4:
LOST

You start. You end. You break. I fell. Into the dark, forever gone.
Bring me back from my grave. I dug it deep, and my heart I gave.
Losing hope. Losing pain. In my mind, it's all the same.
The world goes on, alive nor dead?
Sleepless nights, thoughts of dread.
My soul got lost on this trip.
Hopefully, I find it and keep it gripped!
Tears pour down my face like rain, not stopping 'til the storm
is tamed.
Forever living in a dream. It makes no sense; I don't complain.
The truth hurts when you show the wrong people the right path
to go.
I spoke my words to all my peers, not caring who or what
they'll mishear.
I'm always lost in my mind.
Maybe I'll regain consciousness . . . Hopefully, that I can find.

By: Chantel Rose

I had finally succumbed to the other pressures around me and had
lost my virginity. I felt like a grown-ass adult at that point; I was on
top of the world. I wasn't just in fashion shows anymore but attending the fashion shows and sitting in the front row. I was going to all
the fashion parties afterwards, going to CD release parties, and going

to art district parties. I was bumping and grinding with the rich and famous and had started landing lots of jobs.

My first big editorial photoshoot for a jeans campaign, featured in *Nylon* magazine, was in Montreal. What a gorgeous city; it made me think that if there were ever a city that vampires would reside in, it would be Montreal, beautiful but haunting. The architecture seemed like that of an old world and wasn't anything I was accustomed to. I was extremely nervous on set that day because it was my first big-paying job. I made thousands of dollars that day, just for one full day of work, and I didn't want to let anyone down. The day seemed to go well, the clothing fit awesome, and the look they were going for was working out. So, I put my fears aside after that and learned to relax on set. It wasn't long after that job that I would become known as the chameleon model because I could shift myself on set to look like someone else in each angle. I had become really good at posing.

Some days I was getting paid $150 per hour just to sit there and get my hair and make-up done. I was making killer money and doing something that I enjoyed, although I was supposed to be just a kid in high school. It was an easy job for me: so much fun, so much ease, and lots of money to be made, just in Canada alone. I was so naïve, though; I had no idea how to manage my money and would blow it frivolously. I started partying all night because I had the money, and I could spend that money, and I spend it stupidly. Even though I didn't have to pay for anything when I went out, I did because I could, but then I started to go straight from the party to the photoshoot. Uh oh!

I remember another shoot I had that was a big deal because it was for a trendy magazine, and I was a feature story. I had been out to a artistic release party the night before. I stayed there a bit later than I should've because I had an early start time. My nose was raw, I probably smelled like booze, and my eyes were bloodshot. That day on set, the whole crew knew exactly what was going on with me, but they didn't say anything. It's like there wasn't a problem with what I had done at all. Even though I didn't feel good, I somehow looked good and had shown up despite not having gone to bed. They thought that was a win. I was such a mess that day, and my eye started going lazy mid-shoot; how embarrassing! But we all had a chuckle about it on set, and everyone made me feel so comfortable; it turned out to be a fantastic day.

Now that I look back, what a fool I was to show up like that. What a fool I was to lose my focus on great opportunities just for some devilish fun. At that point, though, I was so wrapped up in the underworld of things that I didn't have a care in the world; I was living the high life, literally. We would go out dancing in the clubs at night, then off to mansions for the after-parties, and everyone was having a ball of a time. It amazes me to this day how everything went down back then. Like, who was driving us around? Who was letting us into the clubs and the VIP areas? Where were the adults to guide me away from my demise? Who were all these people that had so much money? Really though, how were all these people wealthy? It seemed like everyone I knew was rich, besides us new models trying to make a name for ourselves. How old were these people I was partying with, and why was everything just a whirlwind romance, whiplash, rollercoaster ride? I was spiralling down so fast, and there was no one in sight to catch me. I was so caught up in it all I didn't know up from down until I started getting *crash courses* aka the effects of coming down off drugs.

When you've partied a little harder than you should, there's something referred to as a *come-down effect*. The come-down effect can be substantially worse than your regular hangover. When I started experimenting, there were no after-effects because I was young, naïve, and going with the flow. I didn't know any better, and I didn't really feel the effects of hangovers like others did until my friend and I had a conversation one day. The conversation happened after we had ingested a certain substance!

My friend turned to me and said, "Oh, the come-down from this is never good."

I looked at him and asked, "Come down?" I was confused.

He replied, "Yeah, you know where you just feel like hell the next day, and everything is shit."

I replied, "I do not know what you speak of, but that sounds horrible," and I remember him looking at me in shock. He asked, "You don't get a crash after a night of partying; you don't get a come-down?"

Well, you see, it hadn't happened yet, but now that he had made me aware of what the come-down from partying meant, you can imagine what started happening to me on my next trips.

Down, down, down into the pits I go, travelling towards hell and into the unknown. When I say I started having deep depressive episodes from heavy partying, it's an understatement. Before I left for Toronto, on my 16th birthday, I had asked for a cross necklace in the representation of Jesus because of the research I had started doing on him. So, my only comfort during those depressive episodes that pulled me out of the pits of my own demise was that necklace.

I would hold onto that necklace for dear life and asked for help as I twisted and turned in my bed from withdrawals, from the dreaded come-down effect. It was agonizing for me, physically and emotionally. My thoughts were so destructive and hard to control. I felt like I was dying and losing all will to live. I had to find a solution to this problem, but I had no idea where to start. Everyone around me was in the same pits, and I didn't want to be left out of the crowd. I didn't want people to think I wasn't fun. I liked being part of the koolkat scene with all the fabulous parties and famous people I got to hang out with; why would I want that to end? I thought, seriously, who gets opportunities like this, especially where I was from? But it was all just excuses to keep feeding that impulsive, out of control, side of me.

Lucky for me, I had just landed a contract in Europe and thought, *Awesome, a way to get away from the party scene and clear my head.* Ha! I was on a seventeen-hour flight with one other model, not knowing where the fuck we were going. Cigarettes filled the airports, and European accents slobbered away while these people chugged back Heinekens at 7:00 a.m. A few times, I just wanted to stop in and chug back a few of those beers with them to ease my anxiety. Finally, we made it to our destination and, wow, what a culture shock. I was not expecting everything to look so old; it was beautiful but old. Old European to the point that they still flung shit, or whatever it was, from their balconies onto the streets. The hotel we were staying at wasn't great. An older man with a yellow beard—from all his smoking—grumpily greeted us and demanded our passports. I was hesitant and said no and then ran to a payphone to get ahold of my agency to ask why they were taking my passport. My agent informed me it was to make sure the contract time was fulfilled before leaving. That made me very uneasy but it made sense, I guess?

After that, we settled into our room, and it wasn't long before we got a knock on the door. It was two male models, one from Spain and one from Italy, staying at the same hotel for the same reasons. These two men wanted to introduce themselves to us as they got here a few days before and wanted to show us around, but they also asked us if we wanted to smoke hash with them. These two good-looking European models sold us on it, saying it was the best Moroccan hash we would ever smoke. Great! Just when I thought I was getting away from all that, it was getting started again. After that, we hung out with these guys and travelled around Athens with them, but they attached themselves to my roommate and me. So, I started backing away from the one because I was getting uncomfortable with his advances towards me. He was getting to the point of being inappropriate and a little too aggressive when I told him I didn't want what he wanted. At one point, he was so mad at me that he started acting forcefully towards me. There was an incident when all of us were hanging out in one room, and I had told him off for the last time. I was across the room, and he picked up an orange and baseball and threw it at me, hitting me on the side of my cheek! It was so hard, like a full-throttle throw. I assumed he did that because I rejected him. Regardless, why do that to someone? It hurt so bad, and there was a loud gasp that filled the room and then silence; I was so embarrassed. I got up and ran to my room and sat there crying, trying to collect call my mom on an old rotary phone. I was ready to beg her to try and get me home before my contract was up. As I'm holding the phone, praying for my mom to answer, and with the pain still lingering in my face, Mr. Rejected walks into my room and comes' and sits across from me on my roommate's bed. He was several years older than me and several inches taller than me, and he tried to talk to me. He tried to apologize, saying he didn't mean to do that, gaslighting me while trying to excuse his violent behaviour, but my rage was growing with each word he said. He then tried to touch me, and the phone I was still holding onto became my weapon. I just started beating on him with that old rotary phone handle, hitting him in his knees while I'm screaming at him to get out and leave me alone and never fucking touch me again. He left, scared, and left me alone for good after that. Why? Why was it always getting to the point where I felt like I had to fight back for anyone to get the fucking point! Did he not understand the word NO? I'm not interested! Fuck!

It wasn't too long after that when my roommate and I were introduced to a guy who was hired to be the models' host. The host was a well-dressed, professional, who would take us around the city to the best clubs and restaurants. We would be invited to his place to hang out or get ready for a night out, and we would all hop into a limo-type vehicle and hit the best spots in the city. One of the first clubs he took us to was surrounded by cobblestone and old Roman-looking statues and gargoyles. Those buildings seemed to crumble around us only to surprise us when we walked into them. The one club that blew my mind was tucked in a crevice of an alley, which led to the back of the club. I felt like I had crossed into another dimension.

You could not hear the noise from that club on the outside, but when you entered, it was another level of clubbing I had never seen before. There were three levels for club-goers and a fourth for VIP. We were given a tour of all three levels before heading up to the fourth floor. The other three levels played different genres of music and were somehow soundproof, and I can't remember how that was even possible. When we reached the top, we could look through the double glass floor at all the people partying below. There was a spiral circle that went through the middle of the floor all the way down. It's strange for me to think about it because it feels like another lifetime ago. We were treated with VIP status every single time; food and shot platters were continuously brought out to us, and we never had to ask for anything—it was always given to us so freely. It felt so surreal.

At that point, I hadn't really done any heavy drinking because I wanted to avoid the urge to use any other substance, but my room-mate and I dove in deep one night, and you can imagine the outcome. We ended up so wrecked that we were in some random person's house; we had no idea where we were. I was a mess, but I was still very alert. My friend started passing out, and some guys were carrying her into a room; it made me lose my shit. When I say I lost my shit, I am being light about it. I freaked out like I had never done before and demanded they take us back to our hotel. I grabbed my friend and held her up, and went and sat at that door yelling for them to take us to our hotel. All I knew is we were somewhere in Greece; I had no phone, no idea how to call a cab, and I barely remembered how we got there. I just thought, *Holy fuck, what is happening?* I don't remember much after, probably from the adrenaline, mixed with fear, combined with all the substances, but we did make it back to our hotel safely. They did end up getting us a ride, but it makes me cringe to think about it; I was only seventeen at the time, travelling around Europe with people I barely knew. To think back to what could have happened if I didn't stand my ground and act like a complete psycho is scary to me. The possibility of being taken advantage of that night, if I would've woke up to that, I think it would've been bad for everyone. I thank God because I know he was there protecting me; despite my fucked-up state of mind, he was keeping me safe that night.

Finally, the contract was up, and I headed back to Toronto; I couldn't wait to land on Canadian soil. The model party lifestyle was not fun anymore, and I was exhausted from it. I wanted to go back home, and I wanted to see my family. So, back home I went, but, alas, it wasn't for long. I was home for only a couple of weeks before I flew back to Toronto, but it was really nice to see everyone. My friends and family, and other people from my hometown, noticed all the magazines I was in and noticed my face on the billboards in malls. One kid from my hometown was at a city mall when he saw one of my posters inside a Zellers. He went into that Zellers and stole the cardboard cutout right off the rack and ran like hell! Many people were so happy and proud of me for pursuing a modelling career. They were wishing me the best of luck in it and hoped I would go far in the opportunity, but not all of them were so happy for me; I had a lot of haters too.

One extreme example of a hater that got physical towards me was during that brief visit back to my hometown. One night, some of us teens were hanging out in a parking lot across the local bar. Most of us were underage; I was anyway, but the parking lot was a hangout spot for high school kids. Nevertheless, a fight broke out in front of the bar, and I noticed one of my female family members in the fight. These women had lost their shit and were on top of each other like wild animals, and I went over to try and pull them apart to get them to calm down. I didn't get a chance to do anything because out of nowhere, I was slammed from behind onto the concrete sidewalk and repeatedly punched in the face. Specifically, punched in my nose, full force, by a woman twice my age and twice my size. While I was on the ground, not knowing what the fuck was happening to me, I heard this middle-aged woman say, "Maybe this will end your modelling career, you little bitch." Nice. What a friendly world we live in. I remember someone yelling, "Cops!" and seeing the flash of lights, and the woman, who probably weighed three times more than me, pulls me up off the ground like a little rag doll. I just stood there thinking, *Holy fuck, what the fuck just happened?*

The bitch who repeatedly punched me in the face had disappeared. A cop stood in front of me, and his expression told me everything. I hadn't realized how much blood was on my face until I saw how he looked at me, and then I felt it. He told me to clean myself up in the bar bathroom, even though he knew I was underage because of how small our town was, but I was that much of a mess. I went to the bathroom and looked at the damage. Holy fuck. The pain started to kick in, and as I was washing the blood off of my face, that chick walks in and just standing there, staring at me. I felt a calm rage come over me, and I took the blood that was still coming out of my nose, and I walked over to her and wiped it down her white shirt and said, "How does it feel to make a little seventeen-year-old bleed, bitch? Does that make you feel good?" She didn't say a word to me, and I walked out. I had no clue what her intentions were while she stood in the bathroom watching me wash the blood off of my face.

The sad part about the whole situation that hurt me the most was I was there with friends, and they did nothing. Or I should say, who I thought were my friends. Not one of them came over to ask if I was okay, if I needed help, or if I needed a ride home. Not one of my friends came to comfort me. I sat down on the curb in front of that bar, just fuming about what had just happened, and the only person who sat with me was a stranger, someone I barely knew. He's the only one that cared enough to show me kindness after such a hateful thing was done to me. I just sat there thinking to myself, lost in my mind, *What. The. Fuck. Is. Wrong. With. People.* Complicity.

After that incident, I wanted to leave; I wanted to get the fuck away from all that small-town bullshit. I also wanted to go because of the recognition I was getting in the city. I mean, who doesn't like feeling good from being recognized? It was nice to be seen and paid attention to, so I made my way back to Toronto, despite the nagging feeling not to. People were classy, they weren't petty, and they didn't act like hillbillies by getting into bar fights. They knew how to control their emotions, so I went straight back into the wild party scene of the city.

One of those wild party nights ended up with us bringing the party back to our model house. The party was filled with drug dealers, gang members, club-goers, and other models from different sides of the city, who also had their own cuts of the purest snow. At one point, I looked around and thought, *Who invited all these people?* I did. *Who were these people?* No clue. *Like, where the fuck did those people come from?* My dumb ass had invited them. What a mess; my guilty conscience was weighing on me that night. I remember it so clearly. There were lines lined up and down our coffee table; people were everywhere and out of their minds, out of control. One of my close friends and I took a Polaroid picture that night, the old school way of taking an instant selfie. He signed the back of it with the words, "Another time of wasted talent in model search America." I don't even have to look at the back of that picture to remember what it said because it engraved itself into me. The truth about it all at that moment. We were all so fucked up and wasted potential, his statement was true. It was also the first and the last after-party at that model house! It wasn't too long after that when I discovered what that nagging feeling was, which I chose to ignore before leaving home.

A huge event was happening in Toronto, the Much Music Video Awards, and I was invited to that grand event. Earlier in the day, I hadn't been feeling well, and I almost didn't go, but my friend, who was already there, begged me to get dressed and come. So, I quickly got dressed and took a cab to the event, but when I got there, the party favours just started flowing to everyone. Although I had started feeling worse, I ignored it and continued to party, though it was hard to get into the party mood, even with the party favours, and I decided to cut the night short. I remember getting home and sitting on the couch, feeling somewhat spacey and more out of it than usual, and I started massaging my left hand because it felt weird. I couldn't sleep, so I downed some Nyquil hoping it would make me pass out from all the stimulants I had taken at the party. It worked; I passed out cold.

The following morning, I woke up to texts from a friend who wanted to pick me up to hang out for the day. I was still feeling light-headed, tired, and that something just wasn't right, but I got dressed and went anyway. We hadn't been driving for long when I started feeling so sick! I couldn't breathe. My vision went black with stars, my back and chest felt like they were crushing in on me, and I was in so much pain that I not only felt like I was going to pass out, and I did! I remember saying, "I can't feel my hand, I can't feel my hand." I could barely lift my left hand up. He started massaging it the same way I had done the night before; it was giving me a tingling sensation like it was asleep.

After I came out of the painful daze, I was alert enough to ask him to take me to the hospital. He drove me to the nearest one, and I kept reassuring him that I would be fine—I asked him to leave me there, and that I would call him later with updates. I remember a receptionist area was set up outside of the hospital where the nurses were screening people before they could go in because there was a SARS outbreak. They gave me a mask and made me fill out a form to make sure I didn't have any SARS symptoms, and the nurse told me to put the mask on and sit in the waiting room. As soon as I sat down, I started crying uncontrollably; people around me were looking at me while I thought about what was happening to me. I tried to stay awake, and I tried to keep my crying under control when the nurses finally brought me in for tests and blood work. Shortly after, I must've passed out because I don't remember being brought to a private room or having an IV being put in. I woke up, however, many hours later with an IV in my arm and sticky pads all over my body. I was in such a daze; everything just seemed so grey around me. Near me, a nurse was typing away on a computer. She noticed me wake up and asked how I felt; I said, "Better, I guess." The nurse then proceeded to tell me that I had some bad cocktail of chemicals in my blood, and it seemed to have set off a heart attack on the left area of my heart and that I was fortunate. I sat there in shock; I have no words to describe how I felt at that time. She asked me what I was doing in Ontario because I was under a different province's health care system and then asked where my parents were. I said I was here for work and that I was a model. She didn't say much more after that. The nurse then told me that they would be sending me to the Children's Stollery for further evaluation and monitoring because I was still only a child after all. She told me I would be there for a while and that it was my choice whether I called my parents or not. It was my choice to let them know what happened because although I was still a minor, I was over the age of sixteen and for whatever reason, I didn't have to disclose to anyone what had happened. I chose to make the call, and honestly, I don't remember how that call went, but the next time I woke up, my dad was there. When I was released from the hospital, I packed up my stuff and headed home with him for some much-needed rest and healing.

> "Now the Spirit speaketh expressly, that in the latter times some shall depart from the faith, giving heed to seducing spirits, and doctrines of devils; speaking lies in hypocrisy; having their conscience seared with a hot iron; forbidding to marry, and commanding to abstain from meats, which God hath created to be received with thanksgiving of them which believe and know the truth." 1 Timothy 4:1-3 KJV

CHAPTER 5:
LOSING FAITH

Breakaway as it sets, two people in one mind, and you forget.
Which ones which? Your minds a mess, living, breathing, with two
sides that haven't met.
Consumed by fear with only a guess. Which one comes out, and
will you regret?
Being perched upon a ledge at realities cost. Knowing nothing of
it, only knowing you're lost.
Memory function is always the same, never remembering your
given name.
Losing faith with all your friends. Being kept in the present. For
you, it never ends.
Looking for a future that is nothing but gone, with all the little
voices singing you a different song.
You let it consume; I told you not to! Now, what can you do when
your enemy is you!

By: Chantel Rose

My resting period was over, it seemed. I had received an offer to get
into the acting side of things and had landed a contract with an acting
agency in Vancouver. YES! I jumped for joy at the thought of the fresh
mountain air and the ocean breeze. I felt healthy and rejuvenated
again. I didn't entertain going back to Toronto because I was so close
to death while there. I also feared getting back into that lifestyle again,

but Vancouver seemed like a fantastic opportunity and a fresh start. I also missed the whole buzz of being on set and getting my hair and make-up done. I had family and friends who lived there, so it was comforting to know I had some strong ties to grasp on if I needed to, and since I was eighteen—a bit older and a bit wiser, or so I thought— I thought I had a much stronger grip on everything.

Before I had landed in Vancouver, I had my first spot on a show. The day I flew in was the same day I started on the show, so it was a bit hectic for me that first day in Vancouver. My aunt was so sweet, though, because she offered to pick me up from the airport and get me to the studio, in West Vancouver, on time. Which she did, and when we pulled up to the studio, I just thought, *WOW!* The big security gates that said Lions Gates studio on them, the buzzing of golf carts, the lights and different sets that were everywhere for various shows; it was whimsical. My agency had wanted me to get used to being on set and to get a feel for the acting side of things. That first day, I had a simple nonspeaking role to play. I was placed as an extra and as a waitress on the show. I had so much fun and I loved it; the atmosphere of it all was so cool. I felt so happy and back on track with life; I felt like the tragedy of my past was behind me.

After working on set that first day, a couple of guys from the show offered me a ride to where I was staying. Even though it was from strangers, I took the ride. I did work with them all day, and they seemed safe. I felt everyone in Vancouver had such a trusting hippy vibe; it was so refreshing. They felt lighter, more health-orientated, and not so much about the party scene but more about the latest workout routine. I was much more comfortable with Vancouver's slower, more relaxed pace. I had a great conversation during the ride and made two new friends by the time they dropped me off. I stayed with a friend, whom I had known for a few years at that point, who had a loft in downtown Vancouver. He said I could stay with him until I got some things sorted out, which was so very kind of him, but boy, oh boy, it didn't take long for me to walk off that good path and right back into the dark.

You see, although my friend was barely at his place, and I got it all to myself, for the most part, we both had issues. We both had habits of disservice to us, and when we got together, we twisted each other's rubber arms. He and I were both kind and generous souls and were always giving and helping those around us, but one of our biggest issues was using mind-altering substances. It never took long for us to want to be on a different level than our sober realities. Maybe we were always giving away too much of ourselves and not filling our own cup enough like we should've been. So, it wasn't a good situation for me to be in if I wanted to keep myself under control and if I wanted to keep myself alive. The excuses started to consume me again; the fear of dying lost its momentum, but it mostly came down to me not caring about myself. Not caring enough about the life around me to see its worth—to see my worth—and see its true beauty. The seductive thoughts to go against my goodwill were very powerful and sucked me right back into where I didn't want to be.

At that period of my life, I felt like I had a fresh perspective. I felt like I had a bit more control. One night, and in one moment proved that I had gained control over my impulsive nature with my substance use. My friend and I had come back to his place and decided to keep the party going. At a certain point that night, he got called to help a buddy out and told me to stay put. I was alone, alone with my thoughts and in a fragile state of mind. There was only a little bit of our "candy" left, and I felt my anxiety creeping up. What was I going to do? When was my friend going to be back? Ugh! The thoughts that ran through my head. The withdrawal was happening before it even happened! Then, another thought arose as I was internally battling myself. "Substances don't control you; you control the substance. Learn to direct the urge, learn to control the impulse, everything has an energy unique to its self, so learn it, learn to control it, learn to master it."

Now, this probably sounds crazy, and I was probably just high out of my tree, but I will never forget that moment. There are many other moments just like that, not necessarily surrounding the same kind of circumstances, but other moments where clarity arose and guided me through the dark before the darkness had a chance to pull me in too far. I jotted that thought down that night, and there are other count-less thoughts like it which I've jotted down over the past twenty years. These seemingly random thoughts aren't so random at all, and they have been guiding me the best they could from my total self-destruc-tion. That moment was engraved into my core belief system; it helped guide me through substance use and gain a grip on it. Those enlighten-ing thoughts helped expose the shadow lurking within me. The dark-ness waiting to overtake me every time I was too weak to say no. The roaring beast hiding within just waiting for me to expose myself in self-doubt and self-pity. I could see the separation between who I truly was and the darkness inside. I became even more aware of myself and the world around me at that moment, and I was only eighteen.

At that age, I became aware of how deceptive and destructive static thoughts could be and that some thoughts were not your true thoughts; some thoughts were only there for your destruction. I realized, around the age of eighteen, that you have more control of your thoughts than you know and power over the dark whispers you allow into your mind that tempt you, distort you, and that try to take you away from your innocence. I recall thinking, *I will be just fine if there is nothing left and the only power this substance has is the power I give it.* The interesting thing about that statement is that I've come to realize that sometimes people willingly give their power away because they've become so weak, so mindless, and so numb. It's easier to give your power away than to be true to yourself because of all the rampant emotions that regularly overwhelm the mind and body. People have a hard time saying no; they have a hard time processing their emotions, and so they give their power over to someone or something else to take care of it. People like to keep themselves busy and distracted so that they never have to face their demons. People think that giving their power away will ease their burdens, and it does temporarily. What people don't realize is it is never a long-lasting effect, and they keep giving their power away for that slight moment of comfort, but it's an endless cycle of chasing and the more they chase, the more they distract themselves, and the more damage occurs in the long run. Giving your power away only creates more chaos and pain in your life. It only creates a bigger void because of how far you eventually end up running from your true self, and if you've noticed the world around you, some have become too lost to see the destruction of their choices even now. Destructive choices have become normalized, and one could say, even glorified.

So, that night I stopped the chase, my anxiety lightened up, the guilt and shame still hung over me, but the urge to keep chasing a feeling that was never truly there had subsided completely. I was able to rest, I was able to quit, and life became even better in Vancouver because I stopped the nonsense. I had found a group of people closer to my age and had different interests and moved in with my cousins, who were beautiful and warmhearted, patient people, who took me under their wings and became parents to me for a bit. I also ended up meeting a super sweet, successful, and down-to-earth guy who treated me like gold, and things were going very well for me work-wise. I was working a lot and getting noticed by major movie directors, and I had only been there for less than a year. Things were looking up, I felt on top of the world, and things were falling into place to have a beautiful life until I got a phone call.

The person on that phone call was filled with desperation. So much distress, or so I thought, and she asked me to adopt her child. My good nature and emotions towards children have always been to protect and nurture them. I always cared for my baby cousins and babysitting for people before I got my modelling contract. I always wanted to adopt children whose parents had left them behind to show them they are loved. I had even written that down when I was sixteen because that was my goal, to adopt children instead of having my own. I can see now how this person may have played on my emotions by asking me to adopt her child. Everyone knew how well things were going in my life, and I know what jealous people are capable of.

This woman, a new mother, my sister, who was older than me, felt like she didn't know who else to ask and needed my help. I was only eighteen, but I was mature for my age and had started to create the groundwork for a good life for myself. My sister begged and pleaded for me to go back home to help her out. Saying she couldn't take care of her child and apparently there was no one else to help her. So, what did I do? I left my picture-perfect life in Vancouver thinking it would only be for a few short months until I figured out what was going on, but nonetheless, I packed up my stuff and headed back home. What was I thinking? I wasn't thinking about myself, that's for sure.

When I returned home, there was a heaviness in the air, and anger lingered in the home I had grew up in. The children, my siblings, seemed to be left in the dark. What exactly was I supposed to do in that situation? I was only eighteen! Was I really going to adopt a child at that age? I did think about it if that's what she felt like she needed to do. I wasn't going to leave a child behind. I started taking care of her baby boy while she was gone, doing only God knows what, but how naïve was I?. Again, why was I even entertaining the thought? How could I adopt her child, let alone any other child, when I was back in my hometown, jobless? The situation was a mess, a mess that woman left for everyone else to clean up, but eventually, the situation did start to clean itself up.

A team effort was created to help care for her child while she had been lured into the dark by her own selfish choice. Free will. It wasn't because she couldn't take care of her child, it was because she didn't *want* to take care of her child. She had let her selfish ways lure her into the dark instead of being responsible for a life—for the light—a life she helped create. The father was nowhere to be found but eventually came along and took on his dad role. It wouldn't be long, though, until he took both parental roles and had to take full responsibility for the whole situation.

During that stressful situation, I met someone from my hometown and fell head over heels very quickly. Hasn't it been said that "the devil has blue eyes"? The blue-eyed man was charismatic, charming, good-looking, and had such an inviting smile, yet there was something so deceptive behind it. He knew how to make an amazing meal and worded himself so well that I fell in love with everything he said. He wined and dined me every chance I would give him. His baiting of me was slow and calculated. Initially, he was so sweet, fun, and laid back, and I never saw a drop of anger or meanness in him.

I was unaware of a lot of things at the beginning of that relationship; he kept a lot of secrets. That smile of his was able to cover the millions of lies he spoke. I was so blinded and consumed by whatever love spell I was under that I didn't see it for what it was, I couldn't see things clearly. I never questioned his age because I thought he was only a couple of years older than me. After all, he looked so young, and I found out too far in the game that he was over a decade older than me, and of course, by that time, his age didn't matter to me because age was just a number. I was in some fucked up kind of feeling I didn't want to let go of—all I could see was him.

A few months after finding out his age, someone disclosed that he had children. Not once did I hear him talk about his children or anyone else talk about his children, even though I had hung out with members of his family. No one said anything. We had been together almost every day at that point for months! I asked him where his children were and why he hadn't seen them, and he told me a long story that painted his ex as the bad person. My mind started racing. I asked him to get a hold of his ex to see his kids because I was sure they probably missed him but he didn't have a vehicle at the time, so we used mine to get around; we started using my vehicle to pick up his kids. We figured out a schedule, and he started seeing his kids regularly, but then he started leaving me regularly with his kids while he had other things to do. It wasn't too long after that I found out he had two OTHER children, by two OTHER women. What. The. Fuck. Was. Happening. I had grown attached to the two kids I had met and had spent a significant time with them, but everything was just so mind-boggling. I was so confused by all the lies and the deceit.

My confusion led me to talk with my dad about the situation, and I decided to leave that blue-eyed man. There was a catch though, I wanted to wait until after Christmas to do it because we were only a couple of weeks away. I made that decision because we were getting his kids for Christmas, and my parents were so kind and had covered all the costs of their presents for me. I still didn't have a job at that point because I was waiting to go back to Vancouver. I was so blindsided by everything that was happening in my life that time was eluding me. It had almost been a year since I was in Vancouver. Regardless, I just wanted to give Mr. Blue-Eyes' children a nice family Christmas because it didn't seem like they had the greatest upbringing and it was hard for me to think about letting them go. I also didn't want to create a situation that could potentially ruin Christmas for them, but was that all excuses to stay in a bad situation? Or was it the truth? Probably a bit of both.

Another profound moment in my life was about to happen, and I remember it like it was yesterday. It was December 22, 2005. The blue-eyed man and I were sitting on the couch when he put his hand on my stomach and said, "I'm gonna put a baby in there," and he laughed like it was the funniest joke. I remembered I laughed uncomfortably and then became silent. My thoughts were starting to go off: *how someone could think about having any more kids when he didn't even want or take care of the ones he had?* His comment was insane! Why would he want to have another child? Why would he want to do that to another woman? Or neglect another child? Why would he want to do that to another child, a child that would be left without the proper nurturing care of a father? *Why, why, why?* I was disturbed about the joke he made, and I had about enough; it was almost time to break it off.

It was finally past Christmas, and I was relieved that I was about to be able to break that bond, but it was so hard to break. He had a firm grip on me, and he knew it. I may have seemed to have gotten in control of some areas of my life with substance use, but this was not one of them. Who knew you could get withdrawals from a person? Who knew you could be intoxicated and skip out on reality from being in a relationship with a person like that? He truly was a master manipulator. Yet, the bond I thought I was strong enough to break couldn't be broken. I fell for more lies, for his empty promises to be more honest, and that he wouldn't keep any more secrets from me if I just gave him another chance. We were pretty much living together at that point, so I caved. I stayed, and then I decided to enroll in college because it didn't seem like I would go back to Vancouver. I was trapped in a world of bullshit, and it wouldn't be long until my will to live crumbled where it felt like there was no return. Trapped.

"There are six things that the Lord hates, seven that are an abomination to him: haughty eyes, a lying tongue, and hands that shed innocent blood, a heart that devises wicked plans, feet that make haste to run to evil, a false witness who breathes out lies, and one who sows discord among brothers." Proverbs 6:16–19 ESV

CHAPTER 6:
THE DEVIL'S TRAP

Am I a liar? Am I obscene? Look at yourself, look in the mirror,
what do you see?
Your heart is black! Your stare is cold! You're in denial of how
much power you really hold!
Block out the past as you put on your mask! Face reality now; if
you don't, you won't last!
My manipulation, my games, you were over your head, and now I
am to blame?
Your future is gone! I dare you to run! Where you goin' to go when
it's just gettin' fun!

By: Chantel Rose

Nineteen years old and pregnant, Mr. Blue-Eyes' joke wasn't a joke after all. I was pregnant by someone who already had four children with three different women. What was happening in my life? I then found out his friends and family had made bets about how long it would take him to knock me up! Do you see the world we live in? I didn't find out about the bets until after I was pregnant, and hearing them didn't help ease the emotional storm I was going through. I then understood the weird comment his friend had made, "That guy could knock up a brick wall." What kind of sick joke was this? My life had felt like it had become part of a sick twisted joke. While everyone was laughing at me, I was suffering in silence, sitting in tears. A teen that was pregnant with a child. My world was spinning. I had just started college too, and I was only in my first month. I thought, *Come on, already! Life, what's your deal?* Holy fuck! Maybe it wasn't life, though. Perhaps, it was just me and my decisions.

Mr. Blue-Eyes' promised we would figure it out and that everything would be okay. I trusted him; I was so young and naïve. We informally got engaged, and he bought me a beautiful engagement ring, but then he started changing. He was getting abusive, controlling, and dictating. He started getting jealous of my dad and any other close relationship I had with any other male, including my cousin. He also got jealous anytime I went to hang out with female family members or friends. He became possessive. It didn't matter what I did; he always found a reason to demean, degrade, and belittle me.

I slowly started disconnecting from everyone, and on top of all that, my morning sickness was crippling to the point that I couldn't get out of bed. My days were spent dizzy, unable to eat, and staying close to a bathroom because of constant nausea. I was so sick and weak that I had to quit school. Then the cheating started, and some nights Mr. Blue-Eyes stopped coming home. One of those nights, I felt so alone and was in such a deep state of depression that I contemplated suicide. I thought about how fucked up the world was and how cruel people were to one another. How no one gave a fuck about the damage they can do to others from being so selfish and so careless about other people's lives. I didn't want to bring a child into that kind of unjust world, and I was willing to take us both out of it! I didn't know what else to do. I was still just a kid, and he was over a decade older than me; he had the upper hand, and I was in his control, weak to his commands and abuse, feeling trapped.

The day I went into labour, I had to sit in a courtroom with Mr. Blue-Eyes' for hours because of whatever scheme he had gotten into. I was so uncomfortable, and my cramping came in waves, but I put on a straight face and eventually we got through the docket. After he was done in court, I told him we had better go to the hospital. I wanted to call my mom and have her there with me, but he said he didn't want anyone else in the room. He told me that it was supposed to be a moment for just him and me. So, I listened, like a good little girl, and away we went to the hospital; it wasn't long afterwards that we welcomed a baby girl into the world. I remember looking at her in awe; I was so happy and proud to be a mom, but then I would look at him with disgust as he had passed out and was sleeping like a baby on my small hospital bed, taking up all the room. He hadn't even asked if I needed help before he dozed off and as he dozed on the comfort of my bed, that I had recently given birth on, I went over to corner of the room where a rocking chair sat.

Craddling her as I walked around the room and soothing my new-borndaug's cries; I went through the cycles of feeding her, soothing her, and rocking her back to sleep. I found so much comfort in her falling asleep in my arms while I rocked her in the rocking chair. There was so much love and warmth connecting us to each other. I also remember how sore it was to sit down, even with the soft padded pillow the nurse had put on the rocking chair for me. Ouch! I hadn't thought about how giving birth would be so painful or how agonizing and prolonged it would be to heal. Young and naïve. I was so exhausted but felt a new strength growing within me every time I looked down at my little girl. God's gift wrapped up in a soft pink little blanky.

Finally, my family was allowed in to visit. They came in with flowers congratulating us and cooing at the sweet little bundle of joy. Someone took a beautiful picture of me cradling my daughter close to my chest, where my cross necklace hung, glistening from the light of the flash. I wore that necklace not because I was a religious person—I didn't follow any doctrine—but because I believed in God. I believed the teachings of Jesus and the necklace was a reminder of who to look for when I felt alone, lost and needed strength. I strived to walk the good path like Jesus did, and although I sinned a lot, I still tried. I believe Jesus truly is the son of God, who lived in the flesh, and who had the strongest faith and purest love and understanding for humanity and for our creator, our Father. I practiced patience and forgiveness and always looked for the good in people instead of all the bad. I always looked for other's potentials instead of looking for who they actually were because that's what Jesus would do, right? Jesus looks beyond sin and sees the beauty behind the beast. Again, I say that necklace was a reminder that I could find strength and protection in Jesus whenever I felt lost, scared or alone, but sometimes I would forget that and not look to him for those things, and I would forget that He was there for me.

With the birth of my daughter, I no longer felt lost. I felt a purpose rise within me, a purpose full of responsibilities. Soon I would have to leave the comfort of the nurses to the true and hard reality of mother-hood. I may have found strength in becoming a mother, but I was so distracted by the problems around me that I was really moving from one issue to the next, with no real solutions. I was usually focused on cleaning up or dealing with other people's problems as well. Alas, it was time to go home with my beautiful little baby girl and all of my consuming thoughts.

The strength growing in me to leave that blue-eyed devil was on the rise, and I started looking for jobs to find a way to take care of my daughter by myself. He was beginning to project his abusive and neglectful patterns on our daughter, and I wasn't going to let that bullshit happen to her, especially since she was only a baby. I had a growing amount of evidence of his abuse towards me: physical, psychological, emotional, and mental. He didn't have to treat me the way he did, but he did it anyway. Free will. Power of choice. Then the most severe incident happened, and the courts granted me an emergency protection order, having him removed from our home. I felt hope, I felt safe, and I felt strong. At the time, I was twenty years old and a new mother, looking forward to a newly single life.

There were not a lot of jobs in my town, and I wasn't accustomed to making small amounts of money, so I found a job that was over an hour away from my home. I started working full-time and the days were long, about twelve hours from the time I left home to the time I got back, but I was making a lot of money, so it seemed worth it at the time. I worked in sales at a car dealership and enjoyed my job, and I learned a lot. The most challenging obstacle for me was that my daughter was only six months old, and I struggled to find childcare for her. Most daycares only accepted children after twelve months, and most day homes were already full, so I was put on a waitlist. In the meantime, my daughter was being tossed between whichever family member was available at the time, but I was compensating them generously for their help. Mr. Blue-Eyes' had disappeared after the emergency protection order was put in place and that helped keep him from abusing more than he already had. Atleast, that thorn in my side was gone and things seemed to be going reasonably well. Until it wasn't.

I started feeling burnt out, and my family was becoming over-whelmed by my long working hours while watching my daughter. The twelve-hour days, six days a week, one week and five days the following week that I was working had left little room to do much else except come home and take care of my child. Wake up, work, pick up my daughter, sleep, repeat; I was burning out so bad. My family became upset with my irregular hours and any requests I had for wanting time to myself or time to go out with my friends. They never had a problem with telling me how they truly felt, even if it was nasty and unwar-ranted. I was so frustrated; didn't they know I was trying to do my best to manage it all? Couldn't they see I was trying to make a good life for my daughter and me? I was always looking at the good in people and forgiving them for treating me horribly, yet I felt that people only looked at the faults in me, even though I was doing better than others. My anger started to grow. I started getting infuriated, and my anxiety rose. The deep regret I had of leaving Vancouver to help a selfish person with their life and now be stuck as a single mom in this town weighed so heavy on me. I felt like I was suffocating.

I finally caught a break, though; I found a dayhome that would accept my daughter at her young age. The catch was that I had to make it work, somehow, with my crazy schedule; in sales, you always have shift work. My schedule was from 8:30 a.m. to 4:30 p.m. one day, and the next day was 1:30 p.m. to 9:30 p.m. My grandma was the only person I hadn't asked for help, but one morning while having coffee with her, I spilled my dilemma, and she offered to babysit the nights I worked late. My grandma was godsent to help me, and she still is a godsend for me today. She took so much pressure off of me back then, but I had already started bursting at the seams. I was getting sloppy in my mind; my focus and drive were leaving me in my volition. I was beginning to get back into old haunting habits. I started to drown myself and take myself back out of reality any chance I got, which wasn't often, but I felt heavy from the guilt and shame that would consume me after a night out. The critical voice in my head telling me that I was a shit parent and my child deserved better. That voice followed me around everywhere I went. There was no escape. I felt less and less and less. I had no self-worth.

As I reached a new low point, I was surprised to receive some court papers from Mr. Blue-Eyes. He suddenly wanted access to our daughter and was fighting for custody, yet he never offered to pay for any child support while I was caring for her myself. When I think about it, was it really for him to gain access to our daughter? Did he actually want to take care of her? Or was it another one of his schemes? It seemed that he found a loophole to communicate with me without breaking the conditions of the protection order. It makes a person wonder—seeing as how he had taken no responsibility for his other children—why bother with this one?

At that point, I was feeling crushed under the responsibilities that I was juggling and felt ready to throw in the towel. I had started self-medicating, and I was losing the joy of being a parent, which had once given me the strength I needed to leave a toxic situation. I was dying inside again; the light was burning out. I went to the doctor for help, who did not discuss postpartum depression with me, although I now realize it was probably part of my extreme feelings. I didn't know about postpartum depression; no one talked about it, but a prescription for Paxil became my new friend. Where there's a problem, there's a pill, remember? Paxil was a friend that made me believe all was well in the world when it really wasn't. I tried to stay away from that prescription after realizing how just "okay" I felt about everything. There was no happiness, there was no sadness; there was just a weird robotic calm. I was just existing. I was very aware of how I felt on Paxil, and I told myself that I would rather feel the pain than play pretend and feel nothing at all.

After a particularly stressful day of talking to lawyers about the process of the family court system and getting in shit at work for having a meltdown because I was so tired and on edge, I came home and screamed and cried into a pillow that was on my couch. For some reason, I felt the urge to rip that cross necklace off of my neck, and I threw it out of sight. I was so upset and needed someone to blame, so I started to blame God. I kept wondering why He was letting horrible things happen to me over and over again. It was driving me to the point of insanity. What was I doing to deserve all this? I didn't abandon my child; I was doing everything I could to keep us afloat, and yet I kept drowning time and time again by circumstances surrounding me. I asked God, aren't you supposed to be an all-loving, caring, and protecting, merciful God!? I was so mad at Him that even if He had responded, I wouldn't have listened. I felt like I was sailing on a sinking ship, and no matter how well I patched it, it wasn't going to stay afloat. Every time I thought there was light at the end of the tunnel, and I thought things were getting better, I would be sucked back into the dark. That day, I stepped back from my belief in God and felt a numbness come over me. I started retaking Paxil, regularly. I began to feel nothing, and if I did feel something creep up, Paxil was there to push it back down. Problem solved, right?

I had started missing work to go to the court proceedings and would have to see that blue-eyed devil that caused me so much grief with that shit-eating grin on his face. It had been over six months since I had seen him, and I just wanted the whole thing to be over. I agreed to less child support than I could've received and agreed to a convenient schedule for him. I didn't care. I just wanted to be done with it, and then, after all that, the guy started skipping out on his weekends! After he cried to the courts, saying that I wouldn't let him see our daughter, he was skipping out! He could've at least paid the child support amount he asked me to settle with, but he wasn't even willing to help with that! Come on, already! My hate was growing. The restraining order was about to be lifted, and I didn't have much fight left in me, and he knew it. As soon as it was lifted, he started back with his charming, deceptive ways, coaxing me to him. He had his excuses on why he couldn't do this or that and how it would be easier on all of us if we were just together as a family. He would call and ask me about our daughter and start love bombing me during those calls. He started to stop by randomly. Not to take our daughter overnight or anything, you know to give me a break and spend some time with her while I was there. He wouldn't give me any child support, but he would buy things for us that I needed, offer to cook me dinner or take us out to do something together as a family. If there was an excuse to see me or talk to me or do something with me, that blue-eyed devil would find it. The honeymoon phase within the cycle of toxic relationships was about to commence.

Eventually, I caved. I was lonely, depressed, numb, and just wanted the love-bombing to be genuine. I just wanted to be loved. Well, it wasn't long after all that bullshit that we had decided to get back together, and baby number two was on its way. The toxic cycle repeated itself: the cheating, the lying, and the belittling of me. The only difference was that I had a different energy. I didn't care if I was nice anymore, and I didn't care about being forgiving or patient. I started to do what he was doing; I started to fight back and started treating him the same way he treated me. In a strange way, I became stronger.

Mr. Blue-Eyes and I finally parted for good after I started feeding him his own medicine and reflecting to him the shit he put on me. Shortly after our son was born, I said, "Fuck it, I'm out. I'm done for good. Be here for our children or don't because I don't fuckin' care anymore!" And you know what? Life started going well again; I did feel strong in a strange way. I began to not give a fuck about much of anything, except for my kids, and I thought I enjoyed it. My kids are truly my pride and joy, even though I want to rip my hair out and jump out of my own skin sometimes because of them.

Nonetheless, I couldn't get away with not caring about them, even if I wanted to, because there was constant guilt and shame over my parenting that I felt to my core. That guilt and shame kept motivating me to do the best I could for them and be that force for them because who else would? Not their dad. Who else was there to guide them? Not their dad. Although the shit and abuse parents tolerate from their kids is like no other, the unconditional love you feel for your child—to the depths of your soul—should help anyone keep going, no matter how hard life gets. In the end, they need you, and you need them, and we all need each other, but the wounded creatures we all seem to be like to torture eachother.

I felt internally wounded, heartbroken, by my inner critic, created by the constant criticism from their father and the people around me. The judgmental voices telling me what a piece of shit parent I was and saying that my kids deserved better. Yet, I was the only who was there, who was constant, consistent and doing my best. I think that voice is there to regulate us sometimes, to separate our egos so we can know true self-worth and love. That inner critic helps teach us discipline and discernment. To force us, through the deception, to see which voice is true and which voice is false. Took me a long time to feel the truth and know how good of a mother I really am but it took a lot of sifting and sorting through the false judgmental and critical voices before I did. That dark sinister voice can be quite the liar, but you have to determine what's the truth and what's the lies. Are you what it says you are? Or do your actions show otherwise? Don't ever lie to yourself either, because there are always areas of improvement. You have to have an honest conversation with yourself to find out what those areas are. I wouldn't want to silence that voice; it shows me where I am in my emotions, it shows me what I have to work on.

Regardless, my love for my children and my desire for them to see the world better than I did was my goal. I wanted the best for my kids and I wanted to protect them from what was happening to me, internally and externally a lot externally. They didn't often see me upset or cry; I have a good poker face. Every day I would scrape together what I could of myself to look presentable to them. I had written a little note to keep my head above water that said, "If you can't be good to yourself, be good to your children." I was constantly beating myself up, and there was a colossal storm within me that I was battling to control daily, but learning to not care about many things was helping. I was numb, but I needed to do what I could to show my kids the beauty of the world around them and within them.

I was doing the best I could while that blue-eyed devil had moved on to another victim, which was shortly after our son was born. I was off the hook for good, but there was still a beast watching me, waiting for me in the shadows. A covert narcissist ready to pounce.

> "For it is not an enemy who taunts me—then I could bear it; it is not an adversary who deals insolently with me—then I could hide from him. But it is you, a man, my equal, my companion, my familiar friend."
> Psalm 55: 12-13 ESV

CHAPTER 7:
BETRAYAL

Beware of the moment they give you a label that's not true.
Nothing more than a game that you can't commit to.
A scary play, whatever they deem to occupy your whole day!
They don't know between right or wrong, and they trust nothing
but their sorrow song.
They pierce your heart with their rumoured remarks, all because
you try to play smart.
But you can't play smart when they make you play in the dark.
They can't see the encouragers they need to be, free of their
own complicities.
You now cower afraid because you know they're digging you
a grave.
BUT
A switch is flicked, and you feel reality click. You forget the negativ-
ity that was there!
You're going to make sure your life is spared!
The abusers have been stripped and now stand bare!
SO
You freely walk tall and start breaking down all the walls.
But keeping notes on everything and everyone who's false.

By: Chantel Rose

Jealousy, anger, resentment, and vengeance are hellbent emotions.
These emotions can drive people to do the most horrid things to others
in disguise of righteousness when really it is self-righteousness. We
have all done wrong things throughout our lives, but most of us do so
unintentionally, and sometimes these unintentional wrongdoings end

up hurting someone, not just ourselves. These wrongdoings are usually out of a person's own stupidity and mindlessness; they're completely unaware of the consequences due to lack of common sense or whatever it may be. Still, it is never intended to hurt someone else on purpose and always comes with sincere apologies for the pain they may have caused after realizing the error in their actions. These types of people learn from their mistakes, so they do not repeat them.

Then there are the types of people who like to create misery around them because they are miserable. They do horrible things to others with the intent to hurt them; they want to hurt those around them on purpose. They get a kick out of it. They feel better about themselves from it. They relish in the power they think they have over someone by trying to bring them down. Then they pretend to be the victims after they've attacked someone viciously. They cry out with such depth that victims end up believing they deserved what the attacker did to them. They gaslight you into thinking you are the problem and justified their actions. These are the narcissists of the world, covert and sly. We all have narcissism in us, but most of us know it's there and reign it in when it shows its ugly head. Most are ready to apologize for any wrongdoings. If my trail of abusive situations wasn't enough, why not throw a few more into the mix!

I tended to put a lot of burdens and weight on my shoulders because people always put their shit on me but I held it for them, I held space for them in hopes they would become strong enough to hold it on their own but as you can tell it never worked out well for me. Then there are the people who take the weight that is on their shoulders and project it onto someone else, intentionally to hurt them, because all that matters is easing their stressful load for a moment by taking it out on you. It all becomes an eye for an eye because no one is caring about another in the way they should. Where does an eye for an eye lead? Has anyone noticed the amount of narcissism in the world today? Probably not because most people don't even really care to know themselves on that deep raw level. The level that takes the ego out of the equation for a moment and takes you out of your self-righteous wants and impulsive behaviour. Maybe that is why the world is in chaos today!

The type of people who intend to hurt others, yet play the victims, are blinded by the brutality of their own negative thoughts and darkened emotions. They start finding comfort in the lies they tell themselves rather than seeing the truth of it all. The truth for them would be too exposing, and they could never have their hypocrisies shown for what they are, in fear of embarrassment and of humility. It took me years to figure those types of people out, the covert narcissists. The people who I thought were the closest to me were my biggest haters. They were jealous of anything I did because they thought I was better than them. I never made them feel that way about me, like I was somehow better than them. My track record in life wasn't the greatest, but somehow they felt inferior. I assumed it was because they had a hard time containing their dark thoughts. The dark shadows that lingered within them were ready to pounce on anyone who threatened their fragile reality. Those I trusted were just looking for ways to hurt me intentionally with any vulnerability I showed them.

I met such a person who was blinded by her own bullshit and hollowness; the log was in her eye. Her schemes were with vindictive covertness, and I always forgave her for the smear campaigns, the lies, the abuse, and the gaslighting. I forgave her for the backstabbing, for the conversations I held in her confidence, which would come back to humiliate me. I forgave her when she would blurt out my secrets in front of a crowd, leaving me to muster up what was left of my self-worth to keep my head held high. I would pretend to laugh at myself because the crowd she created laughed at my life. It was like she couldn't help herself; she was just waiting for a moment to embarrass me, and sometimes she twisted stories about me to make herself look good while I was the one out of control. She also didn't bat an eye when she put my children in harm's way. More than once!

One incident had crushed me for some time, but I had forgiven her for, though I have never forgotten. It happened years ago, and the memory has been waiting to be released. It was a seemingly innocent night out with her and the person I was dating at the time. My date and I decided that we were ready to leave and, whom I'll refer to as C.N. throughout this story, was supposed to be getting picked up from the new guy she was dating. My date and I left to pick up my kids from my grandmother, who was babysitting, but we ended up going for a cruise down the highway in his brand-new car. We arrived a little bit later than we should've, but this is where everything gets fucked up.

We arrived at my grandma's around midnight, and my son was the only one who woke up, so my grandma suggested leaving my daughter to sleepover at her place and just getting her in the morning when she woke up. My grandma only lived a few houses down from me, and it was a warm summer night, so we just walked with my son over to my place. As we walked with my baby boy and tried to soothe him back to sleep in my arms, we noticed a truck outside my house. Before we had left my grandma's, she mentioned she saw a truck drive around a couple of times and noticed it parked in front of my house but then leave. She thought it might have been us, but clearly, it wasn't. I told her it was probably someone at the neighbours because they had a few roommates, so I didn't think anything more of it. I should've thought a little more of it!

Suddenly, three guys got out of that truck along with some chick I hadn't quite identified yet, and they attacked us. They blindsided us and specifically attacked the guy I was with without him having a chance to defend himself. He was knocked out in that first punch and was beaten and kicked while lying on the cement sidewalk. I could hear him making some weird gurgling sound, almost like he was choking on his own blood, and he wasn't moving because he had been instantly knocked out. I had my son in my arms, and I tried reasoning with the guy who was kicking my date. He then grabbed my arm and shoved me, and I fell to the ground, dropping my son! I screamed at that point, and my neighbour came out to see what the hell was going on. I picked up my baby boy and made sure he was okay, and then asked my neighbour to take him back to my grandma's so he would be out of harm's way. I then tried to push the attacker away from my date, but was restrained by this male in the group, who held me down by my wrists.

I thought this guy had no moral conscience, and he just kept booting my date while he lay lifeless on the ground, helpless. There was no logic to what was happening. My anger was growing, and I felt helpless, but as I was freaking out, I saw who was standing by the truck door in the shadows. That covert narcissist, C.N. The person I was with not long ago; the person I thought was my friend. She stood there with a smirk on her face. I managed to break free, and I charged after C.N. with my fists ready to swing. All I wanted was to wipe that nasty smirk off her face! I head-butted her so hard that I split my eyebrow open when I met her mouth. I mean, seriously. She brought three men to my home that night, three men I did not know! She showed three strangers where I lived, where my kids lived, in the middle of the night; she brought danger to my home!

What seemed like forever, my neighbour finally came back yelled at the attackers, threatening to call the cops. Thank God because I don't know how much more I could've handled. It was really two against four, but technically it was one female against four in that fight because my date had been knocked out from the start. Those assholes took off quickly, and I sat down on the concrete and tried to wake him up. I got him up, slumped him over me, and brought him into my house, laying him on the couch. He had no idea what happened, and really neither did I, other than we were just attacked for no reason. He was completely bloody and bruised, and he couldn't remember a thing—he was knocked out cold. There was no reason for that to happen; it made no sense! Horrible thoughts ran through my mind; I was so upset, and I went back out to look for her.

I didn't know what I would do if I found her, and I am so grateful that I didn't find her while in that rage because I would've been in trouble. Although people like that are justified in their brutality, they don't feel guilty about anything they do that hurts others. They only feel the things that hurt them, and when you see them cry, they only cry for themselves. Narcissists!

When I had time to process what happened, I started making excuses for C.N. I tried to think of what had possessed her to do something like that. The only thing I could think of was C.N., and the guy I was dating, had an issue from the past, but it seemed like everything was resolved because we were all hanging out together. Then I asked myself, *What the fuck did she tell those guys? What did she say that possessed those guys to do something that crazy?* I still don't know, and to this day, she has not apologized or ever said why she did that to us. I would like to know what lies she told them that got them so riled up that they sat and waited at someone's home! To attack people walking, a mother with a baby in her arms, with ZERO warning! I thought, *What the fuck is wrong with people and with me to keep giving those nasty people more chances to hurt me!*

Who goes out of their way to intentionally hurt others like that? I used to ask myself these questions, but I don't anymore because I have the answered. I see people for what they are now, not for who they could be. I don't have those rose-coloured glasses anymore, and my tolerance is thin. It's very dangerous to see the good in people when it's not there, and I realize people are really good at pretending they're something when they're not. I know the good that gets drowned in all the demons because I've lived it, and I've chosen to face them instead of pretending they're not there. People can pretend all they want, they can fake it for a moment with me, and maybe I'll play along, but I can see clearly now.

After that situation, C.N. created a smear campaign about me. She convinced people that night was my fault. She turned some of my family members against me like I was the attacker, that I was the deranged and dangerous one. A family member even called me and screamed at me through the phone, asking me what the hell was wrong with me. C.N. could easily manipulate the people around her with her victim mentality and suck them into her delusions. I may not know, to this day, why it happened, but I see it for what it was, and so do the witnesses that were there that night, even if some of them want to continue to lie to themselves.

I did get in trouble for that night because that covert narcissist twisted everything around on what had happened. She used to make me think the horrible things she did to me were my fault! There is never a reason for anyone to do that to another human being. She has never come clean about what she said to those guys that night or why they were even there.

She continues to convince people of many things that aren't true, which is destructive. Her twisted stories and lies are catching up to her, though, and I can see it through her self-destructing habits. She tries to bury the lies she's conjured with intoxication. She doesn't drink to have fun anymore; instead, she drinks to forget. She will be an even-sadder soul when all her lies come to the surface for judgment, and so my heart does go out to her because I know it comes at a heavy price. I can only pray that she sees the truth of it and forgives herself before it's too late. She has never apologized with any sincerity and has gotten away with too much over the years because of the mask she wears. It was tough for me to forgive her after that incident, but I did. I did it for myself because I wanted peace in my heart, but you can only poke someone for so long before they snap. My forgiveness was growing thin because, year after year, there was something else that she was trying to do to hurt me, and the most pitiful excuses came with her abuse.

Another incident I remember all too well was when she showed up at my house early in the morning, around 3:00 a.m. I didn't have my children that weekend and had fallen asleep on my couch while watching a movie with just my housecoat on. I woke up to the sound of someone breaking into my house through a window. I went to my bedroom and heard a person's voice talking to other people. I immediately recognize the voice; it was C.N! I was instantly pissed off that I was just woken up to her trying to break into my house, and it set me off. I was even more infuriated about it all because I had the weekend to myself to sleep in. As a single mom, that didn't happen often, and I had been looking forward to some well-needed rest. I went to my front door and opened it, asking her what the fuck she was doing, trying to break into my house! She casually said, at 3:00 a.m., that she had left something on my table that she wanted. Seriously, at 3:00 a.m.!? Why couldn't it wait until the next day? I was so pissed off because of how rude she was that I told her to fuck off and to get it in the morning. I told her to never break into my house again, and when I went to shut my door she grabbed me.

I had my one arm wrapping the housecoat around me, and she caught me off guard. I wasn't expecting the whole situation to turn violent. When you tell someone to leave your property, a normal person would, wouldn't they? You would think they would say to themselves, "Yeah, maybe they're right. I shouldn't have come so late, and I'll come back tomorrow." Regardless, C.N threw me to the ground as I tried to keep my naked body covered, and I curled up on the porch while she started punching me in the head and kicking me. She was with two other people, a male and a female, and I think they were equally surprised at the attack. They tried to coax her to go, and they pulled her away from me. I got up and said, "What the fuck is wrong with you," and proceeded to go into my house and shut my door. When I closed my main door, I could hear her come back up the stairs of my front porch. She then started slamming my screen door as hard as she could, yelling through the door some nonsense before she finally left. Like, Holy fuck!

I barely got any sleep that night. When I got up the following day, I assessed the damage. Parts of my screen door lay broken on the ground. *Great*, I thought, *just one more expense to add to my list*. One more thing I would have to pay for because of someone else's fuck up because someone else was able to get away without paying for their consequences. One more incident I would have to try and let go of and forgive. It took me too long to see through her and what she was doing to me. How many times do you let someone betray you and hurt you before you walk away? It was too many times by then, yet I continued to let her stay.

All the lies I didn't even know she was saying about me until they got back to me via the grapevine and then she'd say, *"oh, that's not how I meant it, that's not what I said, I'm not a vindictive bitch."* She would pretend to be there for me in my most vulnerable states to only take the information she got from me and use it against me somehow. She started accusing some of my friends of things and, again, twisting in such a way that what happened to her was somehow my fault. I turned on some of my good friends and blasted them on her behalf, only to see the truth in the end. I was fooled so many times. Eventually, I had enough of her bullshit and I told her what I thought about her, the truth of it all. I started pulling my power back from her and anyone like her because my self-worth was growing. After I called her out, she became very uncomfortable to be around me and sulked back into the silence and darkness around her, finally letting me be.

One of the hardest lessons I've had to learn is that some people who say they love you and want the best for you are the ones scheming behind your back, wishing for your downfall. They do things here and there to try and bring you down; their narcissistic personalities always bring something negative into your life. They try to lower your worth and devalue you so they can keep you below them because people like this think you are better than them. If they can't keep you below them, they like to keep you at their level instead of the level you should be at! I was catching on, though, and now that I knew how narcissists work, I started to play along with their dirty games and ways. Maybe it was time to forgive a little less and give back to them a little more, in a different way. An eye for an eye, anyone?

> "But understand this, that in the last days there will come times of difficulty. For people will be lovers of self, lovers of money, proud, arrogant, abusive, disobedient to their parents, ungrateful, unholy, heartless, unappeasable, slanderous, without self-control, brutal, not loving good, treacherous, reckless, swollen in conceit, lovers of pleasure rather than lovers of God, having the appearance of godliness, but denying its power. Avoid such people. For among them are those who creep into households and capture weak women, burdened with sins, and led astray by various passions, always learning and never able to arrive at a knowledge of the truth." 2 Timothy 3:1-7 ESV

CHAPTER 8:
NO REMORSE

The beautiful life births a child. She sits and watches intently with
a smile.
The smile lasts but a few moments, 'til the horror inside produces
the torment.
Tormented by a brutal force that enslaved her being and took
her voice.
She wants to let us know her hate, but silence captures her
only embrace.
She's castaway to solitude, disgraced, destroyed, destitute!
With a growing life forced inside her, by a remorseless evil with
blind desire!
She gave YOU life, YOU bring her pain, YOU bring her wounds,
YOU bring her shame!
She should torture your unjust, foul soul! For ripping hers out when
she was whole!
Our hell on Earth is rapidly growing. The women and children are
becoming the mourning.
Raped and beaten by unimaginable abuse. All by the hands of the
lives we've produced.
Where is the conscious!? How is it possible!?
That the God of us humans deem us women responsible!

......

Yet, she doesn't know how she has any love left.
She smiles intently as the child suckles her breast.

She buries deep down the torture she felt. Her soul washes away
the torment he dealt.
She embraces the life forced into her womb and takes care of her
pain so she can resume.
The nurturing, caring ways of a mother; to extract all the darkness
so, she may bring life to her flower.

By Chantel Rose

After another lesson in the ways of a narcissist, years went by where I
was in a state of contentment. I was existing, floating through space
and occupying it with various fruitless relationships to pass the time.
Keeping a safe distance from any real relationship, not trusting many
people and not really having any direction to go in, but life was good. I
felt much more confident in life, and I was having a good time. I didn't
care about anything, not because of Paxil anymore—I had stopped
taking Big Pharma's mind-altering substances—but because I didn't
focus on things the way I used to. I didn't put my attention towards
anything negative and caught on quickly to bullshit, so I was able to
avoid it, or so I thought.

I was coasting with the confidence of not giving a fuck. I had landed
a decent job, working in construction, with good pay. I was doing
well for a single mom of two kids. At the time, I wish it hadn't been
like that, but every moment has its purpose. The fact that their dad
fucked off and didn't want to help with a damn thing infuriated me if I
thought about it too much. Instead, the blue-eyed devil thought it was
more important to shack up with any woman who would take him in
than care for his children. Yet, things had changed, and the past was
behind us. Thank God!

I was handling my frustration well and had started reading books
like *The Secret* and listening to whatever was on YouTube about the
law of attraction, specifically Abraham Hicks. I was learning about the
power and concepts of manifestation. These teachings made me think
that I attracted all the horrible situations in my life from my thoughts,

which was a scary concept to understand. If I wanted good things to happen, I had to think good thoughts; I had to be positive and fill my life with positive thinking only. Otherwise, doom was near; things you didn't want to happen would indeed happen because that's the law of attraction. Right? I had an epiphany that it was no one else's fault for their mistreatment of me, and it was only my fault because I manifested those situations into my life. It was my fault because I created my own reality, and I am in power and control of my life! I am the one who manifests all my reality through my thoughts. I thought I had to allow all those people who mistreated me back in BECAUSE I FELT I BROUGHT IT ONTO MYSELF!? I started forgiving people with ease after that epiphany; no grudges, just sloughed it off like nothing. It didn't take months or years; it took moments. I just brush off everything, like what they did didn't matter because I was the one creating it all, right!?

I started some significant momentum from the whole law of attraction and the manifestation concepts. I really did start manifesting amazing things into my life, and those shitty people and situations from the past were like a foggy memory for me with little to no emotion attached to them. I was attracting good people, good work opportunities, travelling worldwide again, and my kids were happy. Mr. Blue-Eyes was picking up his parental responsibilities slowly but surely. Life was good, but another strange feeling came over me through this newfound perspective. The things I felt guilty about doing before, whether it was partying too hard on the weekends or becoming overly aggressive in a situation, I was starting to feel guiltless about it. I was beginning to believe that those who hurt me deserved shit and abuse if they weren't willing to change themselves. I didn't care that I was becoming like the monsters who had abused me: not caring and not having empathy for those with victim mentalities. I felt that I should treat others how I wanted to be treated, or else I'd be playing an eye for an eye with you. I was quickly able to forgive others and forgive myself because it was my fault if I brought on that negativity. What others did to themselves was theirs. My thought was, *Let's all have some fun and take control of our lives because ain't no one making your life hell but you!*

From what I was learning from the law of attraction, I could feel that a different leaf was turning in my life. I started practicing control of my negative thoughts and redirecting them to positive thoughts. I started feeling freer and lighter. I started writing down goals, and amazing business ideas were just coming to me, so I enrolled in a course on public relations. I aced it and then took a business course to create a business plan. I was working steadily and saving money, in hopes of buying my own place, as I had been renting my grandparents rental property for a few years already and wanted to have a place to truly call my own.

My kids were happy and thriving, and we all seemed to be enjoying life. I didn't feel like I was scraping by anymore. I felt confident, strong, and empowered! I barely had any worries. After all, I did not give a fuck about most things because I knew that I could change it with my thoughts in an instant. I was manifesting things that I wanted quickly. I was carefree, and other people's problems weighed no concern on me because that was their shit. I thought, *Maybe they shouldn't think the way they do if they didn't want to be bringing that negativity into their lives.* Not giving a fuck gave a person a certain level of power. A certain level of confidence. Little did I know that I was playing with the devil in his playground.

From the time I had ripped off my necklace and stepped away from my belief in Jesus and God, the devil stepped in to show me his illusions. His magic show, his greatest deceptions of all time. I was unaware of it because everything was going so well! Life was good, a little frustration here and there but almost zero anxiety and a clear mind. I felt as free as a bird until I got a brutal reality check. I believe God came looking for me to wake me up from the illusion in a fatherly tough love kind of way.

I thought I was in my prime in life. I raised my kids with very little support from their dad besides some financial help and taking them for the odd weekend, but I was thriving. It felt satisfying to provide everything for my kids on my own, for the most part anyway. There was still some frustration in doing everything on my own; it would've been nice to have a partner to share my life with; I was still very vulnerable even though I felt so confident and content. Still, I needed a wake-up call. I needed to bring up all the unhealed traumas that I had shoved deep down and never truly healed from. I had to come face to face with it all, and so a man, like I'd never known before, was about to put me to the test. I had known the creep for a few years from bumping into him at a couple bars and parties. We were part of the same social scene. I knew his reputation towards women and how vulgar, mean, and abusive he was, and I stayed away from him for the most part. I had stayed away from any serious type of relationship until him, and I can't even say it was a serious relationship because there was no real commitment. Still, it was fucked up!

I kept straight and narrow and just focused on developing the business idea I had and organizing my finances for the bank to buy a house. I wasn't going out much, keeping to myself, manifesting positive things through positive thoughts and just feeling good about life. I had such a focus, but I knew I needed a slight break. There was a music festival going on twenty minutes away from where I lived, and I decided to just say fuck it for a couple of days and go to party like a rock star, guilt-free, of course. All I can say is, holy fuck, what a weekend it was! I had so much fun, but somehow, the creep and I paired up that weekend and partied together the entire time, not leaving each other's side often.

I was having so much fun, but towards the end, I was just not feeling it anymore, so I stopped the party and went to bed. Alone. I was excited to get back to my kids and refocus after a wild weekend away. Yet, it wasn't long after that the texting began, I had given the creep my number, and he was so persistent that I finally agreed to hang out with him again. Then we were hanging out almost every day. Not even a month later, he got his mom to bring some of his shit to my house. He didn't ask me if that was ok, he just barged his way in, and I let him. I remember catching part of what his mom said when she showed up. It was something along the lines of "What kind of skank are you shacking up with now?" Nice. So his mom approved of him going around using people? And she could just so easily judge someone because of what she knew about her son?

Anyway, what a fucking idiot I was! What the fuck was I doing letting him just push his way into my home like that, with no serious discussion beforehand? Red Flag. I chose to ignore all the red flags and let him into all parts of my life. I didn't realize how desperate I was for that family dynamic until I started putting up with so much shit and abuse. I lived in la-la land, believing something that wasn't. It was super fun in the beginning, and he seemed to treat my kids well. He seemed to get along with all my friends and family, but more red flags started to show, and I continued to ignore them.

The creep and I were partying a little more than we should've been, and one weekend, I was kid-free, and we had a bunch of friends over at my house. As we were standing in the kitchen having a good time, he makes a bet with me! His bet: that he would have me knocked up in a year. Sound familiar? We had only been dating for three months when he made that twisted bet, which I didn't accept and just ignored. We were both fairly young still, and I told him that night that I didn't want any more kids and to look elsewhere. I mean, we were partying that night, and everyone was under the influence, so I just brushed it off and put it in the back of my head. I just wanted to have fun. Besides, it was my life; I was in control, I created my reality, so he can't knock me up; there's protection for that! Right?

With all of those red flags starting to show, I just let myself be led blindly by the creep's bullshit. I asked him about paying rent or helping with bills because he didn't offer to do any of that on his own, yet he was living with me. Any decent person would provide something! Any man would provide for his family without being hassled to do so, and he claimed that we were his family! He was eating the groceries I bought, showering with the water I paid for, and keeping warm under the roof I was paying for. I felt like he needed to fucking pony up; my patience ran thin, and I started to see through his and my bullshit. The rose-coloured glasses weren't so rose-coloured anymore.

I told him that he had to pay $600 a month if he wanted to stay because he needed to pull his weight around there, and being an adult meant that he needed to be responsible. Especially when he tried to rule the house like he was the master of it. Disgusting. He argued with me about paying rent and came up with all sorts of excuses. I was paying $650 a month to live in a basement room at the age of sixteen. The $650 in rent I paid per month didn't include my food, and he was going to argue about paying his fair share to live in a whole house. He was also in his late twenties, but apparently, he didn't know any better and clearly didn't understand how to be responsible! *Holy fuck*, I thought, *what was wrong with him?* What was wrong with me for going along with his bullshit? Why did I keep letting him treat me like that? Why did I have to take care of an adult kid?

Hallelujah! He left for a few months to travel overseas. What a relief! Maybe he would forget about me. Perhaps since I manifested him into my life somehow, I could manifest him out. Yet, he called me every day, and every day I answered. Every day my thoughts were surrounded by him. It was kind of heartwarming that he called me like that, even though he was with a bunch of guy friends travelling across Europe. I started to think that he missed me so much because he's calling me every day, all day, to check in on me and see how I was doing. How sweet. Maybe he wasn't so bad after all and just needed to be shown how to be responsible, and things would be better. How delusional of me!

As I reflect, I question whether those phone calls were a level of control to handle his insecurity since he always asked what I was doing and who I was with. When he was home, he had closer proximity to me, so less insecurity for him. Was he really checking in on me because he genuinely missed me? Or was it something else? Red flag. He ended up leaving his trip two months early to come back to me because he said he missed me so much. How endearing. I picked him up from the airport and thought, *Wow, what a mess,* but I guess that's what happens when you bounce around Europe, especially Amsterdam. He was partying harder than he should, and it showed, but I was happy to have him back earlier than expected. After being single for so long, it was nice to have someone to sleep with at night. Another "adult" in the home was comforting. We were happy to see each other, and away we went into another honeymoon phase, and all seemed to be well.

Christmas was approaching, and the kids and I were getting excited about it. I was getting thrilled to have that complete family feeling at Christmas. It felt so lovely to think about waking up with him on Christmas morning and enjoying coffee while the kids opened their gifts. Christmas would have been our first major holiday together. Well, those thoughts were all fluff and delusional, holy fuck! We didn't even make it to Christmas before the first significant physical abuse began. Our relationship had only been going for a few months, but I guess the roaring beast within the creep could not hold back anymore; his true colours were about to show. The signs, red flags were all leading up to the first brutally violent moment, but as you know by now, I ignored them. I always ignored them. So ignorant I was! I want to mention that all the times it got extremely violent between the creep and I my kids never had to witness any of it. Thank God! I mean, they were there for many arguments but never for the physically violent and extremely abusive episodes.

A few days before Christmas, the creep lost total control. My fantasy bubble about that lovely family-orientated Christmas morning burst. What seemed like any other night out turned into a violent mess. A group of us had gone to the local country bar, and one guy, who we knew well enough to be sitting at our table, asked to play doubles in pool. So, my girlfriend and I got up to play pool, not thinking anything of it, just having fun with everyone. We were all having drinks together, and everyone seemed friendly with each other, but apparently, not everyone saw it so innocently.

The night was ending, the bar was closing, and the creep and I left the bar to go back home. Everything seemed ok, or so I thought. My kids weren't home that weekend, so we had the house to ourselves. What should've been a relaxing bedtime ended up turning into quite the nightmare. The creep started talking about the guy my friend and I were playing pool with. The He used an aggressive tone of voice and tried to create an argument that I didn't feel like having. The creep also played pool with the same guy, and he also had drinks with and talked to him. So why was he making such a big deal about pool?

I asked him what the big deal was, and he started rambling, not making any sense, so I made my way to bed and just ignored the drunken talk he was making. Then he started calling me a slut and a whore as I'm crawling into bed, I just wanted to go to sleep. I'm like, what? I was just so confused and then climbs on top of me in a forceful way and tries to sexually assault me while he's calling me all these names. I asked him, "What the fuck are you doing? Get off me!" I had to struggle to get away from him. He started to chase me, but it was wintertime and I was only in my underwear, so I didn't really know where to run to. He chased me around my house, yelling profanities at me and threatening me. I have never been so scared in my life; it was nothing I had ever experienced before. I had no clue how he snapped like that. It's like the creep went from zero to sixty on the psycho scale. It was an experience that reminded me of the monster he is and the monsters that lay dormant in people who are just waiting to pounce!

At that point of my life, I had never been emotionally, sexually, physically, and verbally abused all at once. He caught me so off guard! I was trying to run to my back door when he grabbed me by my throat and slammed me against the wall next to the basement stairs. He starts punching the wall beside my head, calling me names and calling me by his ex's name; he was in a blind rage. The drywall was breaking by my head and falling to my feet as he wouldn't stop punching the wall, but thank God it wasn't my head. I was stiff as a board, scared, confused, and just trying to think of a way to escape. He then went to the knife block, that was just behind him on the kitchen counter, and grabbed a huge knife from it, and proceeded to put it right in my face while threatening me, saying he was going to kill himself or he was going to kill me.

I don't remember much of what he said after that, but I calmed him down, so he put the knife down. When I felt he was calm enough, I then tried to make a run for it to the front door, and I knocked the Christmas tree over on the way, but he caught me again. He threw me on the couch and struck me so hard that my ears rang, and my jaw felt out of place. He was somehow holding me down with his knees, and I couldn't get a body part free—or maybe I was frozen in fear. I cried and looked away from his blank stare, seeing my cell phone sitting not far from where we were. I must've just thrown it on the couch when we got back, thank God. I started talking to him in a soothing voice, saying we could figure it out and that I was so sorry for playing pool with that guy. I said I wouldn't do something like that again.

The pain started kicking in once everything started calming down. My jaw was throbbing and getting swollen from where he hit me, and I still had the weird ringing in my ears. Finally, I calmed him down enough and he got off of me. I was able to maneuver my way to my phone without him seeing what I was doing. I told him I had to go to the bathroom and get my clothes on because I was cold. He just sat there, with a dark, hollowed, blank stare, like nothing had happened. I got in the bathroom and called my mom, whispering to her that I needed help. I hadn't even thought about calling the cops.

My mom sped over, and when he realized I had called her, he erupted in a rage again. He started yelling obscenities at my mom. When my mom told him to leave, or she would call my dad, the creep threatened to hurt her and my dad. My mom stood her ground, and the creep left. I was devastated; I was so hurt and so broken. I kept thinking, *Did I do this?* How the fuck did I manifest this situation into my life? I couldn't help think that it was my fault, especially when other people downplayed what happened: his friends and his family. They made excuses for him. Although they saw the holes in the wall and knew his past better than I did. I felt they were hiding his abusive ways. They said it takes two, and they made me out to be the bad one; that it was my fault on how he reacted. They knew he had threatened to kill me, and yet it was my fault for that? I didn't act like that. I didn't go out of my way to hurt someone. I didn't go into blind rages and attack people with no conscious awareness of it! I hadn't put one finger on him that night to defend myself. How could I have deserved that; how does anyone deserve to be treated like that? I still felt the blame on my shoulders, and I made excuses for his violent behaviour. To this day, he has not apologized for any horrific moments he caused in others' lives, in my life, and is justified in the horrible ways he has treated people and continues to treat people. I see the picture so much clearer now! Demons do walk among us in the empty shells where there was once a soul.

Like a fool, shortly after that violent attack, we had somehow found our way back to each other. Mostly because I blamed myself from his convincing that it was my fault for what he did to me, and just like that he was off the hook. With my understanding of the law of attraction, I could forgive with ease, remember? I didn't need apologies because I could forgive without them, and so forgive I did. After he realized that about me, it was just a toxic cycle of abuse, and he couldn't contain his demons with me any longer. He was able to put on a show infront of family, friends and my children, for the most part, but the second we were behind the scenes he was a different person. Dr. Jekyll and Mr. Hyde vibes. We would break up from his explosive episodes, and then I would fall for his lies, and we would get back together again. He was incredible at gaslighting me.

He then started to verbally abuse my kids, especially my older daughter, which weighed heavy on my conscience. He blamed her for the re-occurring arguments between us because he had nothing else to argue about, and he was grasping straws. The creep just loved to cause arguments; misery loves company. Every time a holiday or birthday was coming up, especially if it was my birthday, he would do something terrible to ruin it. One night, he even admitted that he was a miserable person and that everyone should be miserable around him if he had to be. I would ask myself how he could be so miserable when he had so much in his life? What was causing this misery for him? I wanted to know because I wanted to help him figure it out. He was clearly battling something that had been suppressed. Was it child-hood trauma? But what was I fucking doing? Trying to help someone who didn't want solutions! I felt trapped; I didn't know what to do about the whole situation. I felt low self-worth, the feeling of not being worthy enough of a real loving relationship because of how shitty he was always treating me. It was sucking the life force from me, but there came the point that I did start fighting back and his power over me began to weaken.

It was an Easter weekend, and my kids were spending it at their grandma's, on their dad's side. I don't know what brought on the argument that night; all I know was that it ended in violence. I was sitting on the couch, and he was blasting me about something. I had gotten used to it at that point and was ignoring him. I was playing on my phone when he came up to me and ripped my phone from my hand. He then tried to restrain me, pushing me down on the couch. Using his knees to hold the sides of my arms down tightly against my body, he squished into the cushions. He put so much pressure on my body that it was hard to move and hard to breathe. He then spit on me, calling me a cunt and all sorts of names while punching me in the chest, knocking the wind out of me, all while yelling in my face.

I hadn't reacted violently yet, but that would come to an end. I wiggled an arm free and started clawing his face, scratching him where I could and grabbing chunks of his skin. The damage I inflicted was painful enough for him to get off me and stop hitting me. Then there was a face-off, holy fuck. I stood there, against a man—well, what was supposed to be a man—and he wanted to go toe to toe with me! Really? I just thought, *Come on, life. Like really, really . . . am I going to do this?* I guess I was! I fought tooth and nail and won the fight that night, almost knocking him out. Almost. We had destroyed the place; my stuff was broken everywhere. As I assessed the damage, he came out of his daze—I had thrown my body weight into smashing his head to the ground from a chokehold I held him in—and it was safe to say that we both had enough of that fight. I started bawling and ran to the bathroom. He followed me and begged me to forgive him! Wow, I had to win a fight for him to apologize to me. What a sick fucking game he was playing!

We showed up to Easter dinner at his family's house the next day. I was unscathed from the parts you could see, but he had scratches all over his face. We had bruises on our bodies, but our clothes covered them. I remember one of his family members asking him what happened to his face and neck, and when we both ignored the question, they just laughed and said, "It must've been a fun night." I know his family knew the truth, and for me, that's the worst part. Complicity.

The creep's family knew what he was capable of, and I would later uncover that the abuse ran in his family. He was abused as a child by his family members; the things he revealed to me in his drunken states were sad, and I sympathized. I had witnessed the abusive, violent, and unnecessary degrading comments within that family. It seemed normal for them like that's how things were; they made excuses for their shitty behaviour. They allowed horrible things to be brushed under the carpet and pretended like those things didn't exist, but I saw the blank stares. I saw the dark hollow space behind their eyes, their cognitive dissonance. My family wasn't any better though, we all have skeletons in our closet, and maybe that's what drew us together.

The creep and I had been together for about a year. Oh, that sly creep, who crept into my home like a thief in the night, who just never left, after trying to steal everything! During that period, the amount of abuse I went through made it feel like we had been together for a lifetime. The stupid fucking bet he made, almost a year prior, was about to come to fruition. What was supposed to be a mini-vacation for me, and I was only allowed because it was my cousin's wedding, ended up being an emotional rollercoaster. I just couldn't catch a break. I felt like I was suffocating, and that part of my brain exploded as I sat there in disbelief of it all.

I had flown to my cousin's wedding, which was taking place on the beautiful pacific coastline, by myself, but I wasn't feeling well. I was just so tired. Although tired and sluggish, I was excited to see all my family, who I hadn't seen in forever, but something just felt off. I couldn't stomach a glass of wine without feeling sick, and my emotions were off the wall; I was so sensitive and snappy. Then that familiar feeling arose. I thought No! No way! Yes! Yes, way! I went to the nearest store and bought a pregnancy test. Fuck, I was pregnant. I guess he won his one-man bet! I was always the loser anyway, never a win-win for me, it seemed. Okay, that is enough wallowing in self-pity.

I started thinking, *Wait a minute, was he able to manifest this into his life? He did intend to get me pregnant from the beginning of our relationship. He planted his intent in my head.* I thought, *Was he able to do that to me even if it's not what I wanted? Was that how the law of attraction worked?* I started questioning the whole manifestation idea that I had been so fond of with a new growing distaste. For six years, I had no pregnancy scares, and now this, especially after he had threatened—I mean made a bet—that he would knock me up within a year. I was going mental at that point. I was going to have three kids, with quite a gap between siblings: nine years, six years, and a new baby. Fuck. I broke the news to him as soon as I found out, and he seemed happy and only slightly shocked. *Hm*, I thought, *if he had planned this and it's what he wanted, maybe he would change his abusive ways because I was pregnant.* I should not have use wishful thinking; all he did was find other creative ways to abuse me.

When I found out I was pregnant with baby number three, I was helping my dad run his business in our hometown. He had a business in the oilfield and I was doing the hot-shotting (oilfield equipment and pipe delivery with a truck and trailer) as well as sub-contracting, working on well sites as a labourer and running heavy duty equipment. I wanted to make sure I had banked enough hours to receive maternity benefits after the baby was born. I couldn't rely on the creep to pay for anything, so I wanted to cover my bills while staying at home with my new baby. I took on a twenty-four and four shift (you work 24 days straight and you only have 4 days off) up in the bush, in the middle of nowhere, clearing land for oilfiled companies. I was running heavy-duty equipment, working from the end of October to January. I hid my pregnancy from the crew and the company I was working for as I didn't want the company hiring someone else for the job because I was pregnant. I worked out of town, busting my ass and missing my kids, and was already in my second term of pregnancy. The creep, on the other hand, was sitting on his ass IN MY home, I WAS PAYING FOR, partying with his buddies!

He was supposed to be helping with the older kids but wasn't, so my grandma looked after them while I worked out of town. The funny thing was, he was always trying to convince people that he was a family man; yeah, sure, okay, bud. I finally couldn't hide my pregnancy anymore, and I had to quit working that construction job. I came back home, and the oilfield business I was helping with started to go under.

So, I found an easier desk job as a tax accessor office and worked there until I was eight months pregnant. During that time, the creep didn't work or even look for a job; he claimed he couldn't find work because of the economy. He always had an excuse. He would belittle me and make me feel like nothing the second I wasn't doing something, but it was okay for him to do nothing? He kept me on my toes more than my kids did!

During the pregnancy, when I was at home and not working, he would take off, saying he'd be back in a few hours, but he wouldn't show up until days later. The creep would come back so messed up and then sleep all day and expect me to wait on him like a maid when he eventually did wake up. Fuck my life, why!? One night, I was so overwhelmed by the different forms of abuse I was going through, plus my pregnancy hormones, and I just wanted to be comforted, loved, listened to, understood, and feel protected. So, I started to share my feelings with him in hopes he would listen. At that point, we had also found out that we were having a little girl. I tried to explain things from a different perspective other than my own. I asked him, "How would you feel if someone treated your daughter the way you treat me?" His response, "Well, if she was a bitch like you, then she'd deserve it." Why was he here then? Why was I with him? What a twisted world I was in. I cried myself to sleep that night, and he didn't have a care in the world; he slept like a baby. He was justified in his abuse.

Our beautiful baby girl was born, and it wasn't long before the physical abuse started ramping up again. One time I was covered in so many bruises that when my sister questioned it, I brushed it off like it was nothing because I was starting to feel like nothing. The abuse was becoming a normal everyday thing. One weekend, the creep's mom had babysat for us overnight, and we had some people over, but I wanted to go to bed. Of course, he started his bullshit. We were in the bedroom, and I was screaming for him to get off me and leave me alone; I just wanted to sleep. I yelled out a specific person's name, the creep's cousin, who was staying at my place that night to come to help me, but my screams fell on deaf ears. I then learned that they were all scared of him too. That's also why it was brushed off like nothing; no one really cared to step in, everyone saw it, but they brushed it off like it was nothing. The creep could be quite the showman, another person in disguise, pretending to be the victim in all his crimes.

Another cycle of abuse was about to end, though. God works in mysterious, soul-altering and mind-opening ways. It was my birthday, and the creep had some friends over at my place. The place that I owned! I wanted to go out, I mean it was my birthday, and he said he would stay at the house with his friends and watch our daughter while I went out with my friends. So, I went out and had some fun, but it wasn't long before the texts started, "Where are you" and "When are you going to be back?" Ugh! I asked a sober friend to drive me home, he was an acquaintance of ours that we had hung out with before, so I didn't see the problem asking him for a ride.

As we drove to my house, the creep was standing in the driveway staring at us as we pulled up. The person who drove me started to get out of the vehicle, but I tell him that I was not getting out because I was scared. I had seen that blank-black stare before, and I knew where it was heading. My sober driver said he was staying out of it, and he headed into the house where the small party was, but I stayed put in the truck. Then that black stare came around the truck to my door and opened it, trying to yank me out, but my hands gripped the handle that was attached to the dash. He was swearing at me and calling me names and finally was able to yank me out of the truck. I started fighting back, then went to walk away and leave, but he grabbed me and threw me into my neighbour's garbage cans, splitting my leg open.

Holy fuck! It was my birthday, and I was a drunken mess stuck between some garbage cans in pain. Happy birthday, Chantel. The creep then puts his hand out, pretending to help me up, only to help me up to punch me in the face and knock me down again. You can't make this shit up. Yet another birthday ruined by him. I was shaking, feeling defeated; I said to him, "Enough. Please, just stop. I'm not leaving. I'll come in the house. Just give me a minute to get myself together before I go in the house and see everyone." He agreed that I should get myself together because I was a mess. No one came out to try and help, as if no one heard the yelling and fighting happening outside! It was a hot summer night with all the windows open. Complicities.

As soon as the creep was inside, I called my sister to see if she was still out and if her boyfriend could come to get me; she said they would. I didn't know that my sister's phone wasn't working properly, so she had me on speaker. Her boyfriend just happened to be sitting with the cops at his truck window, being questioned about drunk driving. The cops heard everything I said when she asked me what was wrong because I was crying on the phone. The cops were familiar with the creep and his ways, and they knew where I lived. They raced to my house after they heard what I said. I had no clue the cops were coming until they were there, but thank God they came. They walked up the back deck stairs and asked me permission to go into my house, and I said yes. The creep put up a fight, but these were two big police officers, and they weren't fucking around. They slammed him against the wall, handcuffed him, and away to jail he went. I was relieved. My sister's boyfriend kicked his friends out, and I sat there crying, trying to give my statement to the cops as they took pictures of my wounds.

An emergency protection order was immediately put in place, followed by a year-long restraining order, but holy fuck, it wasn't over yet. About a month later of no contact, I felt good about the future and got some much-needed rest when I started to have that funny feeling again. I thought, *You got to be kidding me!* Our daughter wasn't even three months old! I was pregnant. Again! I felt like I was going nuts! People thought I was nuts; they asked me why I didn't get an abortion. My reply was and will always be if life wants to be born, who am I to take that life away? I'm pro-life, all the way.

Women are always demonized when an oopsie occurs! A guy has control of his sperm; a woman doesn't have control of it. Men control sperms release! Yet, we look at women like they're the problem of unplanned pregnancies! Fuck that, NO MORE! Why is it that a lot women have to deal with the consequences of unplanned pregnancies alone? Why do women have to use birth control to save both parties from unwanted children? Birth controls that have severe effects and can fuck with the bodies' natural chemistry in the worst ways! What do men do to avoid unplanned pregnancies? Why is it always about controlling women and their reproductive health? Maybe all males at the age of 16 should get vasectomies until they can be responsible for a life and then get them reversed! Why is it mostly the responsibility of the female?

Look at the statistics! Males can just walk away from an "oopsie" like it doesn't matter. Meanwhile, females have to keep it together to care for that child, if she chooses, and if she doesn't, how horrible to have to go through an abortion or the adoption process! How do we bring women back into remembering the sacred value of being a mother and that being a mother doesn't have to take away from one's life but can fill life in more ways than they know. How do you get men to appreciate the value of a mother more and the take on that provider and protector role for their child if a pregnancy occurs?

Motherhood isn't looked at as THE MOST IMPORTANT role like it should be. Motherhood should be glorified and appreciated and held at the highest of importance, and mothers should be taken care of and nurtured themselves, but they're not. Motherhood is looked down on and frowned upon. Like you're not enough, if you're just a mom, you get placed on the back burner, you get made fun of for your "mom" body, you get looked down on and criticized for everything when you're a mother. You try your best, but you never seem good enough for those critics.

So there I was, pregnant again, with a yearlong restraining order against the creep who finally ended up in jail for abusing me. How was I going to tell this prick I was pregnant again? I sat in my bathroom for what seemed like forever, looking at that pregnancy test. The nauseating feeling in my stomach that I was going to have another baby by this abuser. I was screaming inside, and then I was fed up! I mean, really, if I had to feel that way, he should have to as well. So, I messaged him and told him I was pregnant and his response was that he was at work and he would call me when he was finished. Of course, it had been a month since we had talked since that last violent outburst at my birthday, where he was arrested and unfortunately released only a few days later. He asked if the child was his, and I said, "Are you fucking kidding me? Why the hell would I call you if it wasn't, but I know it was just another thing to say to hurt me. Trust me, I'd rather have anyone else be the Dad.

I tried to work things out again with him, and he thought the whole situation was funny; he felt so in control. The creep didn't take anything seriously and started joking about raping me to knock me up again. Knock me up right after this next child was born. He said he would keep me tied up and locked in the basement until another baby was born. These were jokes, apparently, but I didn't hear anyone laughing but him. How is raping someone to get them pregnant a joke? Feeling threatened and wanting to protect myself, I asked my doctor to tie my tubes as soon as my beautiful baby boy, baby number four was born. I was going to go under the knife and get a permanent solution to protect myself from his threats, but it makes me sad that it had to be that way. If I knew anything at all, it was that his jokes were really threatened promises in disguise. Although I felt in a more vital state of mind, I was still scared of what he could do. When you can't see the soul in a person's eyes, don't try to help them because they're empty shells that don't offer solutions in life, they only have a black void to suck you into, only misery and chaos.

My level of anger and frustration had grown into a monster, and I started mirroring the creep back to him. At this point we were still lingering in this half in half out type of unstable, miserable relationship, mostly just for the kids. I started giving him blank stares. I began to control the situation and react lifelessly with no morale in the way I was treating him. He wasn't going to get away with much any longer, and he was going to start feeling the pain he had done to me intentionally. Even though I was lingering with him in this vicious cycle still, I testified against him in court but that only resulted in a peace bond, community service, and anger management courses for him. I was pregnant during that trial, and the courts knew it was his baby, so they thought I had gone back to him after the assault and restraining order had been put in place. They didn't realize that I was pregnant when the assault happened and the only reason why we were in contact was because I had found out I was pregnant after a month of no contact.

The courts didn't listen to the truth as they should have, but anyone can see how the court system fails when it comes to domestic violence. The creep should've received a severe punishment!

I needed to figure out how to juggle all four kids and get rid of the creep's ass for good. I may have been pregnant with baby number four, but I would figure out how to do it independently. I would figure out how to thrive—no more relying on the law of attraction or allowing people to just push their way into my life to try to keep me locked in their traps. I was going to become stronger than I had ever been before and find the will to build the best future for my children. I wanted to move away from the abuse with truth, integrity, and willpower that I knew was somewhere within me that I hadn't tapped into yet, but it wouldn't be long before I did.

> "Beloved, never avenge yourselves, but leave it to the wrath of God, for it is written. 'Vengeance is mine; I will repay, says the Lord.'" Romans 12:19 KJV

CHAPTER 9:
GROWING FAITH

Wrenching as the heart constricts. The blood flow stops. The tear
it drips.
Down your face. Down your lips. The salting taste stops to rest.
Inside a body to rid its light. It fights the feeling that has it tight.
Trying to hold on to all it's worth. It makes a way through to smell
the earth.
The veins engorge with life intact. The heart, it loosens, and the
pain retracts.
All the way to the spine until there is another time.
It sits and waits another day to try and take your faith away.

By: Chantel Rose

My beautiful baby boy, baby number four, entered the world, and I felt
more empowered than ever before. There came a turning point, and I
didn't fully recognize it then, of where that strength was coming from.
The strength was more powerful than anything else, and it was from
God's faith in me that was renewing itself. I just didn't know it yet.

Prior to my two younger children being born, I had decided to give
birth at home. I had already suffered enough from the hands of the
abusers in my life, and I wanted to know the true strength that my
body carried. I wanted to go back to the natural elements, the natural
ways of life. I wanted to remember the sacred gifts given to women
through the power of birth. I wanted to work with my body and guide

it through childbirth instead of being told to lay on my back and push. I didn't want to be numbed or put in a sedated state that I couldn't clearly remember the day my children came into the world. I wanted to be the one who delivered them instead of a stranger's hands. I applaud the nurses and doctors who deliver babies daily. I am thankful for their help with my two older children and for helping other mothers, whom have complications or didn't feel like there was other ways to deliver their children. I just didn't feel like bringing my children into the world with a parade of masked people surrounding me when I knew I had the strength to do it myself.

During my third pregnancy, I started tuning in to my mind, body, and soul on a different level, to feel its strength. I felt I was beginning to remember something I had forgotten so long ago. I hadn't worked during my fourth pregnancy because I was busy taking care of baby number three. So, I couldn't bank any hours for another stretch of maternity leave or maternity benefits. Although I felt strong, I was also stressed about my finances. I thought, *How in the world was I going to juggle all the responsibilities on my plate by myself? How was I going to feed my children, especially with no child support?*

At least the creep was leaving me alone, for the most part, because I often wouldn't let him back into my home. The moments I did let him, he sucked me in, and I shot him right back out. I was getting better at saying no, I was getting better at seeing through the lies. I was getting better at creating the boundaries I needed to keep him out for good. It was easier because he wasn't helping with anything anyway, so what use was he other than to be my tormentor? I started looking for a job. The fastest and best paying job I could get was back in car sales. I needed a job asap because the bills were piling up, I was getting no child support, and I just needed something to keep the roof over our heads. The only thing was, my little boy was only four months old. I had to send him off to a sitter for ten to twelve hours a day, sometimes six days a week. Thank God my grandma was there for me again, who also helped my two older ones get to school on time. She also looked after them the nights I worked late. Baby number three had to be shipped off to daycare at the age of one. Again, the grandparents were picking her up for me the nights I worked late. To this day, I regret leaving my baby boy at such a young age to have to go work. I regretted it with my older child, having to leave her at six months to start working, and I see the effects of not having been in their lives for that first year! The strange kind of insecurities of pushing their mother away but always wanting her close. A type of separation anxiety but resentment at the same time. I didn't think my absence would affect them the way it did because lots of mothers work shortly after having a baby, don't they? Aren't mothers encouraged by society, by feminists, to go back to work not long after their children are born? Like I said, I didn't realize my absence would have the effect it did, but I can see the effects of it. My two middle children, whom I was there for at least the first full year of their lives, do not have these types of anxieties. Mothers if you can, please be there for your babies when they are little. Do whatever you can to stay home with them and not go back to work unless you absolutely have to. Something needs to change in society to take the pressure off women. So that they can breathe and remember the truth within them. The truth that keeps being suppressed and manipulated and is driving them insane, to the point they can't remember how to relax into motherhood anymore, instead they want to run away from it.

The creep refused and still refuses, to pay child support because he said I was working and making more money than him, so back to court we went. I was able to get a maintenance government account set up, and they could chase after him for money because I was tired of it. Like the court proceedings for my two older children, yet again, I settled for less money than I should have. I settled for less money because of his sob stories about his finances, but he lied. I found out later that he lied to the court and to me, but I didn't push the subject because it just meant pushing the court dates. Funny how I could waste so much time on terrible people and then settle for less so quickly in court because I didn't want my time wasted. Make it make sense! It was sad because the judge had to force parental time on him as he refused to stick to a schedule. He wanted to pick up the kids whenever. I thought, *What was wrong with a schedule? What was wrong with committing to specific dates to see your children?* Children need structure and balance. A schedule works for everyone; why was he refusing one? It was all just more games, more control, more ways to try and come by my house whenever he liked in the excuse of picking up our kids. The duty counsel finally told me, "You can't force someone to be a good parent." She was right. You can't.

I was six months into my job, and all I wanted to focus on was my career and raising my children the best I could. They were in hockey and dance, and I enjoyed taking them to their extracurricular activities. I was doing good in life again; I felt like I was in a good spot again. I was trying to maintain a social life the best I could—it's nice to feel like you have friends—but then I started to feel burnt out. I could feel myself slipping by the time spring of 2017 came and my youngest was soon approaching his first birthday. Terrible thoughts started filling my head: *why aren't the fathers of my children at least helping financially? Why do I have to juggle all of this myself? Why do I always have to take responsibility for everything? Why do I always have to take responsibility, even if it's someone else's fuck up or wrongdoing? Why am I always the one to bring peace, and be the compromising one, and be the one who always settles for less! Why?!* They made me feel like I was suffocating again, like I was drowning again, like I was empty again. I started to feel like nothing, like I deserved nothing and that my kids deserved so much better than me because of the decisions I had made that brought so much bullshit into our lives. I couldn't juggle that plate anymore; it was overflowing with all of my responsibilities. I was ripe for the taking again because I was losing my focus on my goals. It also didn't help that the harassment started up with the creep again. He was showing up at my house and at places I hung out at with my friends. He was talking about me in negative ways and spreading lies about me to my friends. He started to play on my emotions again after I thought I was done with the prick. I couldn't handle it anymore. I broke. I had a mental breakdown. I was burnt out, and I needed rest. I needed away from it all.

I felt so defeated and like I wasn't good enough for anyone or anything, and I decided to leave. I decided to just up and leave. I left my kids with my grandparents and said I needed to go; I couldn't breathe anymore. I left in a pile of tears with my children standing there, not understanding why. My children never saw me cry, but I could no longer keep a poker face. My grandma knew how stressed I was becoming, and she offered me so much support at that moment as I stood at her front door bawling, and then I just walked out the door. I packed up some clothes and left, not really knowing where I was going. I blocked my abuser from contacting me, and he picked up my two younger children after finding out what had happened. I had to have a mental breakdown for him to be responsible for his children. I couldn't even stomach contacting him to ask about my children; that's how deep into the dark I went. That's how deep I was drowning. I couldn't speak in my defence about anything. I just cried and was alone with my thoughts. I drove into the mountains, looking for solace and looking for peace from the dark thoughts that were consuming me. It took about a week of just being by myself to calm the storm in my mind. It took about a week to start thinking clearer. No one else knew I had a breakdown except my family. To everyone else, I had just gone on vacation until my tormentor, the creep who crept into my home so many years ago, started a smear campaign about me. He told people how I just ditched my children and didn't care about them anymore. How bad of a mother I was. He was preaching his bullshit to anyone who would listen, and some of my friends did listen and judged me for it. I had no fight in me to explain myself. I let them think what they wanted to.

After that week, I started feeling a little hope again. I knew I needed space, I needed to breathe, and I needed the quiet to get ahold of the dark thoughts. I was sitting outside on the balcony of a suite I had rented near the ocean in Ucluelet, BC, when an eagle made itself aware to me. He started flying right above me in circles and then stopped and sat on a nearby branch and just watched me while I watched him. I felt such an overwhelming sense of peace and inner strength come over me. I felt the need to go back home. I wasn't giving up; I was just resting up.

My eldest daughter had a dance competition close to the mountains where I would be driving through on my way back. One of the other dance moms, who was a godsend for me, told me she would bring my two older children and meet me there. It had only been two weeks from when I left, but it had been too long for them and for me to be gone. My two older children told me to never ever leave for that long again, and I didn't. I felt refreshed, but I knew I had to find better ways to cope. I knew I had to recognize sooner when I started to feel burnt out.

When we got back home from the dance competition, I had a hard time unblocking my two younger children's dad to let him know I was back. I still couldn't stomach the thought of him trying to come near me or even talking to me. Eventually, I did though, it was about a week after I had got back that I found the courage to message him. The desire to have my two younger children back in my arms was overwhelming, and I couldn't hold out anymore. He didn't even hesitate to give them back and the transition was smooth, which was nice in thought but was only because he couldn't handle taking care of them for much longer.

They weren't the same children when I picked them up. My baby boy started showing signs of violence: hitting, punching, smashing things, punching me in the face. He was only one. My two-year-old daughter was now timid, reserved, withdrawn, and would curl up in the corner if anyone's voice got too loud. I vowed that I would never let anything suffocate me to the point where I would leave them like that again for that long. I had to start working with my youngest boy to soothe out his violent tendencies and promote hugs and kisses instead of hitting. I had to let the daycare know that he had to be reminded of giving hugs and kisses instead of hitting and smashing things. I had to talk to my little boy in the calmest manner and show love and zero aggression to get him out of the violent states of mind he would get in. It took a long time for my two younger children to trust and feel safe again and show their loving sides. People say not to have regrets in life, but I do, and they're warranted. When you don't learn the lesson fully, history will repeat itself.

Now that I was back home, I had to go back to my job in a male-dominated atmosphere. The car sales industry is chauvinistic; I don't care what anybody says. So, I wasn't being treated well in that atmosphere, even though I was top sales. I had to figure out a way to stay at home while making money. The idea of going back to school then popped into my mind. I thought, *Why not enroll in university? Who cares if I go into a shitload of student debt!* At least I'd have more time with my kids, and I should be able to find a good-paying job with a degree. A psyche degree had the high potential of me being able to work from home. I had always been interested in psychology and had read a ton of books while on my travels as a model. I mean, I wasn't always at work or out at parties. On days when I had nothing to do, I was in a Chapters or some sort of bookstore and would spend hours there, sipping lattes and filling my head with all more information and knowledge. So, the idea of earning a psych degree felt like the right direction to go in. I enrolled in university and started racking up the student debt to keep our heads above water financially. My enrollment went smoothly, but getting back into the groove of things in school, at a university level, was a little tricky but nonetheless doable.

I felt so much relief that I could do my schoolwork while my older kids went to school and while my younger ones were at daycare. At least this way, it was only six-hour days instead of a twelve-hour day where I would be gone, and I was free on weekends so we could do as we please. By going to university, I was the one to pick up my children from daycare and school. I was the one who was able to feed them supper and put them to bed every night. I found a way that worked better for everyone, and it kept me closer to my children. I was still productive even though I wasn't generating a income and only generating debt. I was okay with it since it meant my children and I were closer together while still moving forward. There was all that hope for a brighter future, but I was still reeling inside from those negative thoughts that cause my mental breakdown a few months prior.

Although I was strong enough to continue searching for solutions, I felt such little worth about myself. I was still crushed by how people had treated me and why they treated me like that. I know I'm not perfect, but I would never treat someone the way I was so harshly and unjustifiably treated. I would never go out of my way to cause pain and chaos in someone's life unless it got to the point where I had no other choice.

Although things seemed to be running a lot smoother on the outside, I was still feeling on the inside. The wound was slowly healing but oozing, leaking toxicity into my body and mind. When I felt a burnout coming on, I would get a babysitter and fill my weekends with empty moments of partying. I started having excuses for being out later than I should've. I started doing things I know I didn't want to be doing, but I was content, fuck it. I thought that I deserved to be a wreck sometimes. I had my shit together. My bills were paid, and I was raising four kids on my own with bits of child support that came my way. I thought I deserved those weekends out; people told me I deserved those weekends out. At that point, and again, I was only existing in survival mode, not living or thriving. I had passion in my heart for something, but I didn't know what, and it was frustrating to be searching and never knowing.

The weekends I spent partying was with different faces, but it was always the same. The same conversations, the same types of problems being repeated over and over again. People had their pipe dreams but no solutions; I was living in an insanity loop. There came a point where not only was I feeling sick about myself, but I was starting to feel sick of the people I was hanging out with. I just felt like there was something more to everything, something more than partying every weekend. I started to ask, how many people look forward to that weekend escape? How many people were dead inside? How many people were pretending to be okay when they weren't? How many people are using prescriptions or other mind-altering substances to skip out on reality whenever they can? Where does the problem lie? Why is humanity lying about being so sick?

Everything was so blah for me. No one cared to do any better or be any better. People liked to distract themselves with petty bullshit and getting caught up in competing with each other. I was getting tired of observing it. I was getting tired of people competing with me instead of supporting me. I started to go down the path of not giving a fuck about much anymore, again, except for my children. They were the ones who kept me going even when I didn't want to, they kept me strong enough to correct my direction every time I went the wrong way.

Although I felt little to no worth for myself, I value my children above anything else in this world. I wanted to make sure I could provide for them in the best way possible, even if I was screaming inside. As part of a mother's purpose, it is to protect and to provide for her children, no matter how you feel. You must find a way to overcome the darkness for their sake. Children are the purest lights in this corrupt world, and we must protect them at all costs. The strength my children gave me was potent, but there was a power guiding me so subtly that it went unnoticed for a long time. A pure power that I had forgotten about a long time ago that helped in lead me back to the path I kept choosing to wander from and helped me stay afloat. I would later unexpectedly receive a revelation of this power that surrounded my life, the power in this world, of oneself, outside of oneself, of the law of attraction, and of manifestation.

> "When the righteous cry for help, the Lord hears and delivers them out of all their troubles. The Lord is near to the brokenhearted and saves the crushed in spirit. Many are the afflictions of the righteous, but the Lord delivers him out of them all." Psalm 34:17-19 ESV

CHAPTER 10:
ESCAPING THE DEVIL'S TRAP

You poser! You liar! Consumed by desire. I hate you! I love you!
You lit my emotions on fire.
You promised to take away all my pain! How naïve I was! Now I
realize it was all in vain!
I will capture the moments you stole from me! Harbor all my emo-
tions until it's time to be freed!
I'll cry when you fal
My body still feels the urge to scream! I gave you your happiness
you only felt in your dreams!
BUT
NOW THAT I AM AWARE OF YOUR ACT! YOUR SCENE!
I CAN CLOSE DOWN YOUR LIFE AND WIPE MY
SLATE CLEAN!

By: Chantel Rose

Charles Baudelaire once said, "The greatest trick the devil ever pulled
was convincing the world he didn't exist."(1864, Le Joueur Genereux,
Le Figaro) There I was, back in my not giving a fuck state of mind.
I was feeling confident in it and powerful in it. I started manifesting
again, getting in control of my thoughts again, making excuses for
the people around me who hurt me again. I was easily able to let go
again, brush things off again, just go with the flow again. The only
difference was that I was creating stronger boundaries. Even if people

were treating me shitty, I put up strict boundaries with how much they could get away with. My tolerance for bullshit was getting thin. I started to put my foot down, hard, you could say. Every time I stood up for myself with such conviction, friends and family had nothing else to say or do, except to tell me to get off my high horse. I didn't understand then why they were saying that to me, but I know now. They had no other ways to hurt me because I didn't give a fuck what they said or did. So, these devilish people thought that by trying to pull me off, whatever horse they claimed I was on, I would be brought back to their level. A lowered level where they could make me succumb to their abusive ways again and be buried in their bullshit. They were slowly starting to learn, though, that there were consequences for their actions. If they tried to attack me physically or emotionally, it wasn't going to be fun and empowering for them anymore. I even started asking them to join me on this high horse because maybe they needed to see life from a higher perspective. But I could see how miserable they were in their lives. Maybe it would have made them happier to be on a high horse, but I could see they only became triggered by what I said. So, I just walked away from them all. I took my power back and watched them fall.

Other people, kinder and good people, were seeing the shift in me and acknowledging it, telling me how strong of a woman I was. Considering what I went through, yeah, I guess I was a strong woman, and they only knew snippets of my story. I started to ask myself, *How is not caring about stuff, about the world around me and not giving a fuck— even if it is towards those that have hurt me deeply—empowering?* When a person states this, they're taking away from their life. They're not actually facing the reality of their life, so fuck it, they say. Something didn't seem right about that approach, it felt good, but it was good in a false sense. I was starting to realize not giving a fuck was an excuse to avoid my true feelings, who I truly am, but it was such a seductive way to ignore the truth. Why did I want to ignore the truth? It seems many people don't want to look at themselves to see why they don't give a fuck and they don't want to process their emotions properly. They would rather numb them out rather than feel them, rather than care enough about themselves to create the change they want to make. It's easier for some people to stay in their chains rather than to break free of them. A lot of people have refused to look at what's happened in their lives. They refuse to look at the things that have caused them to drown in their emotions: the things, the people, and the environments surrounding them. It's all fun and games when you're drunk, high, or just ignorant and in denial, but what happens when you come crashing down? Do people want to stay numb, stay distracted from themselves? Or do they want to truly live again?

I want to give you an idea of what I'm talking about so I'm going to use vampires as an example. You all know how seductive the life of a vampire looks like in the movies. They're beautiful, don't age, don't care about much because they're immortal. They have superpowers of all kinds, super strength, except when in the light, and except when it comes to their lusts. They are a prisoner of the dark and a prisoner of their lusts, and of their flesh and bone bodies. Their devilish life-style that seems so glamorous and sexily seductive is how they are able to suck their victims into their traps, through the manipulation of a feeble human mind. This is how movies portray vampires, but is it only in the movies?

The thing is that vampires are dead inside, they may be immortal, stuck in their flesh and bone bodies for eternity on earth, but they are dead inside. They avoid all emotions because if they had emotions that would make them human, instead of the soul sucking vampires that they are they are and driven by their impulses to feed their lusts. During that period, I was living a somewhat glamorous and seductive lifestyle, even while being a single mom. I looked pretty on the outside, but there was a thirsty beast on the inside. Whenever I would feel that beast wanting to be released to go have some fun, I would literally message my friends and say, "time to release the beast, Satan take the wheel". I was trapped in my own dark lusts of the world around me, off and on, and trying to break free of that all the time. Hence, the off/on cycles in my life. You can't break free though if the lights are out and you're not caring about solving the problem. You can't break free when you chose the comfort of your lies instead of the truth. You can't break free when you've handed your power over to something or someone else to look after because it's easier than facing your reality and owning your true, STRONGER power. Seductive manipulation and lies will suck you in every time you're about to come to the light. And no matter how life looks on the outside, it always will come down to what's on the inside that's most important. I was never sucking the energy from anyone either, I have always been and will continue to be a giver to life. Although I saw many people around me who didn't have a problem sucking the life force of others through their manipulations and games, draining them to the point of no return. #energyvampires

So, here's where the law of attraction starts to tie in again. During the second round of the not giving a fuck period in my life, I was manifesting again like crazy. The law of attraction is a real thing and there is nothing wrong from steering your thoughts from negative to positive, but it's teaching you to believe that you have full control of your life and your creation through your thoughts. Like I've said before, the law of attraction is partially why I think I allowed many people, who are not good people, to get away with a lot of things that they should've been held accountable for. I can say they are held accountable now though! It's a dangerous game to believe you are the creator of your reality and your thoughts are what drives your experience. Although partially true, it's not the full truth. It's dangerous to become that self-absorbed and self-centered where you believe you are the only creator of your reality and everyone else is just playing the role you gave them.

I loved the law of attraction because it worked so well for me in materials gains. It seemed to be very easy for me to get what I wanted when I focused properly. I was a poker player, and I always won the big jackpots, thousands of dollars in winnings. I never walked out of the casino empty-handed, and I gave credit to the law of attraction. I kept ignoring my intuition, though, that something was off about everything. I was too intoxicated from receiving everything I wanted, and I dove into the devil's playground deeper, almost getting lost again.

Everything was being handed to me; why would I question it? Why would I want it to stop? Why was something off? I thought I was having so much fun and that the world was in the palm of my hand.

I travelled again: tropics, Vegas, Coachella, LA, VIP Hockey games, and taking my kids on beautiful vacations. People told me they were jealous, and I didn't blame them; life seemed easy for me. While others talked about their struggles in their marriages, in raising their kids, it all looked easy for this single mom of four who had little support from their dads. My life was pretty amazing and seemed so full. So, why was I questioning it!?

I was so confident in my don't give a fuck attitude that I started treating those that treated me like shit, like shit. I matched nasty to nasty. There was no abuse in my life because I started showing a side that scared people. Everything was so good and comfortable. Everything was trouble-free because I didn't let trouble bother me. I was powering up and not giving anyone the slightest chance at powering me down, but I was going about it the wrong way. It was a false sense of security full of lies and illusions to distract me from the truth.

In a clip from a movie called, *God's Not Dead*, two actors, a middle aged man and an elderly woman in a nursing home are having a conversation about God and the devil. The male actor states, "And here you are. You're the nicest person I know. I am the meanest. You have dementia. My life is perfect. Explain that to me." The elderly lady replies, "Sometimes the devil allows people to live a life free of trouble because he doesn't want them turning to God. Their sin is like a jail cell, except it's nice and comfy and there doesn't seem to be any reason to leave. The door's wide open. 'Til one day, time runs out, and the cell door slams shut, and suddenly it's too late." When I came across this clip it resonated with me so much because I could feel the detachment I had in this state of mind I was completely disconnected to my heart and my emotions but I thought I was living my best life in this weird content, detached frame of mind, which was definitely nice and comfy. There is a difference between true calm and peace of mind and numbness and emotional unavailability but they act in the same way. Although they come from two very different places. One is trying to fool you with illusions and one is coming from a place of truth.

When I thought I was at my peak, when I felt myself step into that strange, seductive power, the oddest, and somewhat terrifying, things happened. One by one, the people who lied about me, who spread rumours about me, who were my worst abusers, started having horrible things happen in their lives. Tragedies befell them and their families. A weird work accident left a person handicapped. Others were involved in different types of accidents, major health issues, severe mental breakdowns, and even death. And it was every single one of them. It started as one after the other and I just thought, *Wow, this can't be a coincidence, but what does it mean?*

Once became too many for me, and I started thinking, *How, why?* Many other people in my life were amazing, and I saw their successes grow. Their lives were becoming more beautiful while karma was catching up to, I suppose. At one point, my ex started calling me a witch. I had kept warning him that if he kept treating me this way, karma would pay him a visit, and eventually something came around. One example is from one of my worst abusers, who fell from a 20-foot house in a standing position onto a cement pad. He shattered his feet and heels and lost his ability to walk. He lost his ability to hurt anyone physically, and is stuck in his own physical pain for the rest of his life. For months, he was unable to walk and was bedridden. For months, he was alone in his pain and could think about everything he had done. All of this started to weigh heavily on my conscience. I thought if all of those people had done some terrible things to me, did they really deserve the things that were happening to them?

I wished those tormentors had sought better ways of treating people so they could bypass the pain they now have to endure for the rest of their lives. I never sought intentional pain on my tormentors, as they had done to so many others; I only explained how karma worked and that it would come for them one day. You can't keep treating people terribly without consequences catching up to you. I knew something would happen without me ever having to do anything; all of those tragedies had befallen those liars, betrayers, abusers, and people who had taken advantage of me simultaneously. One after the other, over four years, my consciousness started to shift very subtly, and I felt the essence of something I had forgotten. I also began to think that the law of attraction was sadistic. If I say karma is going to get those who caused so much pain, and if I truly believe it, and it starts to happen . . . uh oh. Then again, now that we have become accustomed and have a fairly strong understanding of the law of attraction, the karmic law is now coming to the forefront for humanities deeper understanding, but that's for another time.

The law of attraction guides you to ignore what you've done that was wrong or the wrong that was done to you and to not give a fuck about it, to just get over it quickly and move on. To just think positively and positive things will happen for you. Like I said this proves true because I've tested it, but there was an emptiness that came with it. The law of attraction literally says you are you pushed out and you are just playing all different roles in your life in basically a simulation you control with your thoughts. Is that it, is that all there is? Really? The law of attraction claims you're able to do whatever you want, you just have to recorrect your thoughts to get more of what you want, right!?

A whole movement began on social media with people feeling the same way I did about the law of attraction. I wasn't alone in this realization that something this seductive was so off. That you can do whatever you want if you can master how energy and manipulating energy works. Is that why "elites" use rituals at Bohemian Grove to stay in power? because they've mastered the manipulation of energy in a nefarious way? How does a small group of people keep control over billions of others? #savethechildren

I had an epiphany that the spirits who come through those that teach the law of attraction were quite deceptive. Quite charming, but nonetheless, deceptive. They offer a great sorcery of manipulation to make you believe you can manifest anything into your life, by doing certain things, and putting aside any negative feelings and emotions. "It is what it is." Be positive and forget the rest because you can change it with your thoughts. The idea is to ignore your pain that you caused yourself or that someone else caused you, or that you caused others because you can change it by saying mantras and writing down positive affirmations. This can make you quite fearful of any bad thought that may come into your mind and may cause you to actually suffer more if you can't pull yourself out of that tailspin of negative thoughts. If a person does get negative thoughts, when aware of this law, then they start working overtime to keep those negative thoughts contained. I realized that people have to have negative thoughts as they have to begin to understand why they have them and such emotions and face them to start healing themselves, instead of playing the denial game and living in a "cell that has open doors." They need to heal the place the negative thoughts are coming from, rather than force themselves to avoid, distract and run from the pain, from the truth of the thought and instead embrace it and overcome it. People don't realize that they have to face themselves, their negative ways, and their demons to ask for forgiveness for their past mistakes. This healing, this change, will fill their cups and keep them flowing instead of never feeling satisfied. When you're never satisfied, you're always craving more, always wanting more.

There was always a missing piece for me, even with living the good life. None of what you have in your life is truly meaningful if you're still just a hollow shell of a person and always having to search for something more. I wanted my life to have meaning, and I started stepping away from the law of attraction and all new age spirituality. I went into that dark hollow shell of mine to look for answers. I was ready to discern between the truth and the lies, the good and the evil, the light and the darkness, and then the real change happened. My impulses were easier to control. All of those guiltless moments I didn't want to feel, I started to feel. I started feeling everything that I had refused to in the past. I started to see all the lies I had told myself; all the denial of how hurt I still was from the people I thought loved me. It all started showing itself for what it was and I started envisioning a completely different life for myself and my children. The veil was lifting, slowly but surely.

I began to remember things from my past, things I had learned, things I knew at such a young age but forgot I knew. I was at a crossroads in my beliefs. I started realizing that I cannot judge and I am not here to deliver punishment. If there was just cause of vengeance, then God's wrath is righteous in his deliverance of justice to those needing to be avenged. I am only here to observe and tell what I see. I am here to seek truth and to help others see clarity through the illusions. I am here to help people who are seeking guidance and forgiveness for the things they've done out of selfish ways, so that they can heal and co-create a beautiful life while here on Earth. I am not here to sugarcoat anything; I'm a sinner and I am here to tell it like it is.

New Year's 2020 was fast approaching. With my fresh perspective breaking through, and although I still felt somewhat lost, I had a clearer path that I wanted to take. I was at a New Year's Eve party with some family and friends when I joked about how bad I wanted the world to shut down so I could quit school, so I could pull my kids out of school to spend more time with them. I just wanted to travel and get back that time I lost with them from all the bullshit that I went through.

Although I was home every day and only had my psych degree to focus on, I still felt like it took too much time away from my kids. I craved that quality time with them so much. I told the group of people I was speaking to at that party that I just wanted four or six months to take off somewhere with my kids, somewhere beautiful, like the mountains. Somewhere away from all the small-town bullshit where it was just them and me. It was only three months later that the mysterious virus hit.

My kids got very sick at the end of November and the beginning of December. The illness would get a little better only to get a lot worse, continuing until the end of February 2020. The doctors had no idea what was going on and couldn't give us any answers as to what kind of virus it was, only that it had to run its course. My children were put on steroids, inhalers, antibiotics, and antihistamines, and I was giving them extra doses of vitamins. Again, we had no fucking clue what was going on. It took until the end of February for it to rip through our family, including our extended family. Everyone got through the mysterious virus, though, including my 86-year-old grandfather, who refused to be hospitalized. After realizing all the prescriptions the doctor gave us weren't working, I started using other ways to heal my children. Along with the extra vitamins I had been giving already, I gave my kids and myself elderberry that had zinc, holistic herbs, sea moss, bladder wrack, garlic oil, and Epsom salt baths with eucalyptus every night. I finally started seeing results from using these natural herbs, vitamins, and minerals, and we all started to clear up. I had only suffered from a high fever at one point for three days and had a dry cough, but that was it. What followed from the mysterious virus outbreak would soon shake the world like no one has ever seen before, but it ended up giving me the opportunity I was looking for.

"No temptation has overtaken you that is not common to man. God is faithful, and he will not let you be tempted beyond your ability, but with the temptation he will also provide the way of escape, that you may be able to endure it." 1 Corinthians 10:13, ESV

CHAPTER 11:
TRUTH HIDDEN IN PLAIN SIGHT

You were an already scripture art before you held doubts.
Perfected on the palm of your hand, your life is drawn out.
Holding a key to all knowing, not having to go afar to seek.
But our minds incapable of seeing . . .
As though looking above for the mountaintop, whose clouds forever
cover its peak.
We grasp at the possible because we know it can be achieved.
But capturing the impossible is feared because we think we'll
meet defeat.
What is defeat? A manufactured lie. So, they can taunt you
of failure.
Laughing . . .
While a million tears want to scream out through your eyes.
No one ever fails if they try! It's only seen as failure through
unfaithful eyes!

By: Chantel Rose

Winter was over and we were going into spring of 2020. On media outlets this mystery virus that the doctors couldn't identify back in November 2019 was no longer a mystery. By the time March rolled around it was being called COVID-19. Is that why Bill Gates hosted the "Event 201" in October of 2019 and handed out stuffed corona-virus "teddy bears" to people at the event? Event 201 was a specific exercise for global government bodies to address the issue of what to do if a coronavirus were to ever be so deadly that it would cause a pandemic. Interesting. Covid-19 was a coronavirus that leaked from a lab in Wuhan China, things that make you go hm, leaked from a lab they say? I mean from a bat? Very interesting.

At least the doctors knew what they were dealing with to help their patients overcome the virus. I was more than grateful to have my family get over the virus before the media and government became involved. By then the media outlets were really starting to create some fear about the virus, not any immune boosting solutions, only fear and restrictive measures. Governments started locking down countries worldwide, restricting travel, gatherings, closing schools and daycares, and shutting down workplaces. *Great*, I thought, *I still have two months of my term left, and although my schooling was all online, how was I supposed to work that out with four kids running around our little home?* Two of those children were only three and four years old. So it was stress time again to try and figure out how to juggle it all out, again. Ugh.

I asked some family members to help me out with my two younger children. I needed to finish my term, so I asked if someone could take them three hours a day, five days a week for the next two months. My grandparents were still recovering from the effects of COVID-19 and it was too much for them to care of both the little ones. Plus, I didn't want to take the risk of potentially exposing them to the virus, again, since we still didn't know much about it. I asked my other family members who weren't working, so I thought they would say yes. I even said I would pay them to help me, but they came up with some elaborate excuses that they couldn't help me at that time. I was really pissed off because I knew what they did with their time, and I knew who they would help at the drop of a hat. Yet, when it came to me, no one wanted to help out. No one was there when I ASKED, but everyone was there when I didn't need them and I didn't ask, but they'd offer up help for the most mundane tasks, where food or beer was always provided to them after. I mean appreciated but not necessary. I felt like certain people were constantly wanting me to fail. They pretended to be there for me, but were they? I felt like they were wanting me to just quit on everything by not extending their hand out to help when I asked for the important things that I really needed help with. It felt like they were rubbing into the wound they know they helped put there, hoping I would cripple and fall and not get back up, holy fuck.

I thought, what the hell did I do in my past life to get shit on so much like this that I can't find anyone to help me out with my children during the week. They all wanted to be there for the good moments, clicking pictures away with all the fake smiles, joining me on my vacations, having drinks with me, just fake as fuck. Like what did I even do!? I wanted answers. People were always asking for my help, asking for my advice, asking to come on trips with me, asking to borrow my vehicle, asking to borrow money! asking asking asking, taking taking taking.Good grief and thank God my pity parties never last long and I do always find a solution to my problems I am solution oriented, seek and ye shall find.

I finished my term because my two older children helped me out with my two younger ones. Shortly after I figured out the school schedule, I realized that my wish on New Year's Eve came true. Like, what?! It was hard for me to believe at first, but government officials did close schools and pretty much everything else. The world shut down. Did I just catch a major break? The break I so desperately wanted so I could spend time with my children? I know that sounds terrible to say at the beginning of a pandemic, but I was over the moon realizing my kids were out of school and I was almost out of school. Who knows how long schools would be closed for, but I would take full advantage of it. I had some money sitting aside from the poker winnings that I wanted to use to take my kids to the ocean and mountains for the whole summer. With the pandemic hitting like it did, it seemed like sooner rather than later was a perfect time. I finished up my last two months of school and planned to leave for the mountainous valley with my children in April. I scored some great rentals for the full month in the most gorgeous places. We packed up and went away. The weather was beautiful, and where we went, everything was green. By the second week of May, the water was warm enough to play in. Every morning I would wake up and make a fresh cup of coffee and just admire my little sleeping beans. I would then walk out onto the deck and enjoy the view of the lake and the mountains. My children and I spent every day at the beach, playing in the sand and going for hikes. I got myself into a workout routine and started tackling my inner demons that I had begun to face. I was snappy a few times with my kids because of all the heaviness I was bringing to the surface, but they made sure to put me in my place every time I lashed out and reminded me of how much they loved me.

My children have helped me realize so many things; they have taught me about myself and life. They make me want to handle things with more grace, love, and understanding, so they never have to go through the things I did. My children have helped guide me back when I felt lost, and during our travels, we were healing; I was healing. I wasn't ignoring my feelings, I was feeling all of them, and by the grace of God I got to do it in God's land. The fresh mountain air and the sweet people we met along the way. It's interesting how strangers can provide so much comfort and relief when the people closest to you seem so out of reach. It felt amazing to get away from the static of the small-minded, small-town dilemmas. I was feeling really good about everything, but I wasn't in the clear yet.

My children and I had been gone for a while and we were dreading the thought of going back home. We didn't want to leave, but then I got a phone call. My basement had flooded from the major spring rainstorms; my sump pump had quit working! Fuck! We had perfect, and I mean perfect, weather where we were vacationing. We had a pool and a hot tub that we went down to every day and relaxed in, and we had nothing but sunshine and rainbows. There had only been a handful of storms, but they didn't last that long and brought magical lightning shows to watch. We had tennis courts and mini-golf and waterfalls, and a beautiful hiking area behind our rented place. Why, oh why, oh why! We were headed back to the pit to assess the damage at a place I didn't want to be part of anymore.

Once we got back home, I could feel people's jealousy behind their fake fucking smiles and pointless conversations with me. It was really starting to show in its full exposure. All the knives aimed at my back;

I was just so over it. People were constantly questioning how I could live life to its fullest with four kids and do it on my own. Like I was involved in some illegal shit. In their minds, a person couldn't create a life like this without doing something bad to get it. I didn't deny any of the rumours. I let people believe whatever they wanted to believe, but I was more boring than they thought. I had been posting our adventures on social media, and they say there are evil eyes out there so be careful what you show. I felt that.

I also felt like something wanted to burst out of me. I was having a hard time tolerating most people. I had a growing desire for something that I couldn't quite place my finger on, and I was actually starting to feel bored and was unable to get into the fun of even drinking and socializing anymore. If I did go out, I had to get so wrecked to enjoy myself. I just wanted to go back to the mountains with my kids and have that peace, have that awareness, have that light start to flicker again. I hadn't felt that since I was a child. Life, though, it happens, not always the way you want but always the way you need.

Shit started going sideways two months after our vacation. People judged me for every little thing I was doing. Jealousy is a helluva emotion! So, I now have a rule for myself that once you start judging me be prepared for me to judge you. I started telling the truth about what I saw in them. The things I kept to myself because I did not want to judge them. The things I let slip by because I didn't want to make them feel bad about themselves. The things they were being hypocritical about and blinded by I exposed , hoping they could see the truth of it for themselves, but they turned their face from it.

I also started to care again; care about the weak and broken-hearted, who sought healing. I thought I didn't give a fuck about any of that, of any of them, except for the small select few, but it turned out that it was just a lie I had been telling myself to mask my pain. I am someone who does care, who loves deeply, and who cares a lot about the truth, justice, and love. Bitterness was leaving me and the truth of things was bubbling up and overflowing no matter how hard it was to face. It felt like I was being released from the hellish prison I willingly put myself in. Free will!

People confided in me with their upsetting stories, looking for comfort. I did not react to them at all. Someone said that I had the emotions of a stone, but I always seemed to give the right advice that made the most sense for them. I was always able to put a light inside their dark, but I had stopped doing that because I thought I had stopped caring. One night, a young girl came up to me and told me something quite disturbing. A group of people I had known for years did something to her, and she said she couldn't remember details, but she remembered enough to know it felt wrong. After she told me the story, my blood boiled. She was so young. Why she told me, I still don't know. I didn't even know her name or who she was, but I knew the people she was talking about, and I really cared about what this young girl was saying. She had been taken advantage of by people I thought weren't like that, and then I felt my conscience kicking in hard. I thought these people were better than that, but really they were predators. They were lost in the dark, but I was so blinded by not caring that I couldn't see things for what they were in full view. I thought those people had more morals, but then I started realizing just how immoral people had become, including myself. I let these people know how I felt. I let them know how wrong it was to take advantage of that girl, which left her humiliated. Their response told me everything I needed to know. They had no shame in what they did and no apologies. So, I let them know I saw their souls and how dark they had become. I started seeing the truth of everything. The veil had been lifted on all those situations I had ignored and I saw it all for what it was, without judgment but with justified anger, with righteousness. I then knew what it meant to be truly justified in righteous anger, and from that moment, something that was once only sparking was now a full flame.

After that, I felt like I needed to go back to my place of peace: the mountains, the ocean. I needed to understand how I felt because I was feeling wasn't anything I had ever felt before. I needed time to reset and sit with these newfound perspectives. To get my head straight because I had spent over twenty years feeling lost, and I felt like I was waking up from a bad dream to the truth. The inner work I had been doing started to release me from all those chains and demons that hid themselves so well within me for so many years. A major purge of my mind, body, and soul started happening and I was flooded with so much of the truth of this world. The truth of things I had forgotten in all the pain and demonizing I did to myself. The truth I had buried in the void I created and had filled with meaningless things. I started to remember the powerful things I had thought of as a child to bring into this world. When I was a child, I had such a passion for life. I wanted to solve the world's problems. Bring more love and light to the world. Show the lies and the injustices of the world so we could truly correct them. I was a very passionate child, and people who remember me as a child will attest to that. Somehow, along the way, I forgot who I was, and that missing link I had been chasing and searching for, for so many years, was with me all along.

> "Finally, be strong in the Lord and in the strength of his might. Put on the whole armor of God, that you may be able to stand against the schemes of the devil. For we do not wrestle against flesh and blood, but against the rulers, against authorities, against the cosmic powers over this present darkness, against the spiritual forces of evil in the heavenly places. Therefore, take up the whole armor of God, that you may be able to withstand in the evil day, and having done all, to stand firm. Stand therefore, having fastened on the belt of truth, and having put on the breastplate of righteousness, and, as shoes for your feet, having put on the readiness given by the gospel of peace. In all circumstances take up the shield of faith, with which you can extinguish all the flaming darts of the evil one; and take the helmet of salvation, and the sword of the spirit, which is the word of God, praying at all times in the Spirit, with all prayer and supplication. To that end, keep alert with all perseverance, making supplication for all saints, and also for me, that words may be given

to me in opening my mouth boldly to proclaim the mystery of the gospel, for which I am an ambassador in chains, that I may declare it boldly, as I ought to speak." Ephesians 6:10–18 ESV

Chapter 12:
A Child of God

The eagle soared above, so high up in the sky, circling me endlessly,
I had to question why.
His stance, his perch, so strong, as he rested on that branch.
But still watching me intently, I felt his message, a second chance!
To be reborn and expand my wings, wider than ever before.
I couldn't ignore this eagle's message, I felt it in my core.
I had to find what I had lost, find a way to restore my worth.
To remember all the beauty, that God had given us on this Earth.
I had to free myself from all those ties that strangled me!
I had to cut those cords that wouldn't let me be!
I had to break through the illusive walls that kept me from
being free!
I had to find that strength and power that needed to be released.
And so, I thank you, God, for reminding me of who I am meant
to be.

By: Chantel Rose

I went back to my place of peace, the mountains, the ocean waves, the fresh unpolluted air on Vancouver Island. I had only brought my sons with me on this trip and it was amazing to just have that close quality time with them because really my girls get a lot more of my attention. While I was there I collected my thoughts to make sense of what I was being presented on a spiritual level. I realized I was always looking at the potentials in people while the demons in them were looking at me. That's why I was always being attacked. Your body makes you weak in battling the physical impulses that surround you. That's where addictive tendencies step in and take over, making it harder for you to battle dark energies that want to take you over on a daily basis. That's where all sorts of other impulses and distractions with stimulations kick in and take over. So that you stay lost in that insanity loop, and your spirit can't gain control because you deny it's even there with all your distractions. Who has faith anymore?

I know I am talking very negatively about the world around us, but if we take a hard look at it and seek the truth underneath all the lies, we can find healing, we can find grace, we can find beauty, and we can find strong faith in the unseen. It is a dark journey when you're seeking truth because you must look at the atrocities in this world in its full context. You cannot look away, you cannot brush it off as less horrific than it is, you cannot deny, you must see it in its full exposure. It's not an easy pill to swallow, but one that eventually has to be nonetheless. That is if you want to take the weight of the lies off your back and clear the smoke away from your eyes. We have been living in a world of great deception. We're constantly being lied to and stimulated to react in certain ways to certain things. Those that have the willpower to control the static thoughts and discern between what the truth is versus what the lies are, are coming forward now more than ever. These truth-seekers are shining a light on the dark, and are overcoming the fear of persecution because they know where their strength resides.

Do you remember in one of the beginning chapters, early Toronto/ Modeling years,where I mentioned about the stories I heard and the secrets I kept about those rich and famous people? I see now, after almost twenty years of burying everything down deep, that it was all the truth coming to me, but I was unable to see it for what it was. I denied those stories I was told, thinking they weren't true. I had a feeling everything was so wrong around me, but I couldn't discern between the truth or the lies of it all. I believed people were just telling stories in their drunk and high states, and they were all bullshit, but as I look back, I was a child surrounded by vultures taking advantage of my innocence, but I thought I was so cool. To me, the fucked-up things they were saying were just because they were off their rockers on drugs. That's the only time I heard such horrific stories was when people were under the influence of drugs or alcohol, but maybe that was because that's the only time they were comfortable enough to tell the truth. Those rich and famous people would tell me things I would brush off because I didn't think the world was actually like that. I was also a teen, a small-town girl in a big city scene and hadn't quite seen the horrors of the world like I do now. Those stories are now relevant more than ever as I reflect and see the truth in them.

One of the stories that stick out for me was a brunch event with some rich people in a ritzy hotel lobby restaurant. We had mimosas with our brunch, of course, and then it turned into day drinking, and while people were up and about socializing with others, I was stuck in a corner listening to some deep shit someone needed to get off of their chest. The story revolved around the Hollywood scene and how they would sacrifice children, including their own, in some sort of satanic ritual bullshit. The person telling me this story was upset because his family member was deeply involved, and he had sacrificed his firstborn to whatever sadistic shit he was into. His family member made it look like an accident—like SIDS. I was taking in this conversation with a grain of salt and thought, *Wow, this person is really fucked up. Who would do that to children, let alone their own child?* This person was just messed up. That was over fifteen years ago, and what are we hearing in the world today? #savethechildren

I used to block out the thought and belief that the devil was real. I didn't want to think that anything I had ever done could potentially send me to hell or that humans were capable of such horrible things. I believe in God, even though I had turned my back on Him. I believed in Jesus, but I wasn't Christian, and I refused to believe in the devil, but little did I know how much the devil believed in me and I definitely felt at certain times sucked up into thatvery seductive energy.

The power in this type of frivolous, don't give a fuck about anyone or anything but yourself, type of energy is intoxicating and hard to leave. Satan's energy provides a kind of safe comfort zone against your real heart-felt emotions. Raw emotions that you should feel in full force and learn to gain strength from, and look to God to overcome when they feel overwhelming. But the devil doesn't want you doing that. Why do you think he distracts you with so much? He wants you stuck in his comfort for long enough until he has you trapped in his sinful ways with him. The narcissistic, violent, soul-sucking energy that Satan is made of up is very real, hell is very real, and people need to wake up.

If you've been paying close attention to the world around you though, people are waking up from their slumbers they have been put in by all the lies surrounding them. People are becoming strong in their uncomfortable emotions, so that they may free themselves of the chains they've allowed to be placed on them. Whether they know it or not God has been yelling at them to WAKE UP! To wake up from the slumber that has made people docile, robotic, wanting nothing but the physical flesh cravings that surround them, the sex feigning, prescription pill popping, alcohol, and illegal drug abusing people trapped in the devil's services. God wants them to wake up now! And turn away from these lusts, from these lies, from these spells, that the devil has cast, with the help of humanity, so that humanity can be saved. The devil has sucked people into believing his lies and it has worked for so many years, until now. The truth is hidden in plain sight; that's how sadistic the devil is, he shows you the horrors of what he's doing but makes you think it's all lies, so you do nothing about it. The devil gets you in a state of cognitive dissonance that disassociates you from yourself, from God's truth, from God's power. God gave you free will; remember that and choose wisely! The mystery virus, Covid-19, gave people a break from the deceitful environment that was keeping them so busy, with the physical aspect of everything, and started to remember how to nurture the spiritual aspect of themselves. Although people were bombarded with fear over the virus, to promote a certain agenda, it actually created the atmosphere for so many people to turn back to God. Those people that forgot how to nurture that inner light, and brushed off the guiding force within, the Holy Spirit, is now being released in its full glory. The virus has given us the space and time to think for ourselves again. To slow down the pace and feel God's presence that we kept denying. Lots of us were able to find that inner guidance, even with the constant fear mongering by the media. For every slick move the devil thinks he has, God has a better one and I was needing help out of the my own personal hell I had created.

I was still caught up in my past life habits from when I was a model. Even though I had gained control of it, and it didn't control my life. I still told myself that drinking and using drugs recreationally was okay to do, and I kept giving passes to myself. I kept making excuses for things that had no purpose in my life, and that numbed me instead of enhancing me. I realized very strongly that I was still escaping my life because there was something I was trying to avoid, even though I started to see the truth of everything. The truth is hard to swallow, and the truth was what I was still avoiding. I didn't think I wanted to give up my old habits, but it all started to feel pointless.

I no longer wanted to drink, but what else was there to do when everyone based their lives around their next drink, their next party, and their next weekend escape? I hadn't fully embraced God yet, and I was still asking myself what was I searching for? What was I truly needing to escape? That cycle of repetitive insanity I didn't enjoy anymore and probably never did. I seemed to have everything I needed; I was almost done a degree in psych, my kids were thriving, and I was thriving. I felt the essence of something that was making an appearance in my life in full force, but I wasn't quite sure what that was yet and then it hit me.

I laid in my bed one night lost in my thoughts, thinking about the world around me, and how things had come to be. I was thinking about the children of this world being sacrificed, being sex-trafficked, being abused on a daily basis. The millions of abortions every day and the other innocent lives caught up in that sick ring of greed by vile natured creatures that imprisoned them. The fears and worries of raising my own children in this fucked up world were haunting me. Thoughts of Indigenous women being murdered and no one batting an eye or Indigenous people from all over the world being treated in filthy ways by the vile bottom feeding creatures of this planet. The rise in domestic violence and rape still rampant as ever before if not more now. Men hating women and women hating men and people hating themselves. People not being able to accept who they were born to be, or the parents not accepting the gender their kids are and all kinds of genders being created to push down the truth of who they are and people just burying themselves in so many lies.

My mind was just racing, going through all these thoughts and emotions and I started thinking what the fuck is the point of all this. What the hell has happened to the world. It was hell on earth and I in that moment wanted to get the fuck off this planet. Like no one seemed to be doing anything about anything. Governments were too caught up in their own bullshit lies against the people, trying to scheme up new ways to control them and keep them in line and just completely fucking useless when it came to solving any real problems for humanity, and I just felt hopeless about it all. I thought about how my life was just one repetitive cycle of bullshit without any real meaning because the world was so fucked up what was the POINT.

My thoughts were consuming me into a black void, and I felt completely hopeless that night and I started to cry uncontrollably. I was so tired of it all, and I didn't even realize how exhausted I was because of all the lies I was still denying. I couldn't swallow that truth pill, and I was exhausted. I didn't want to carry the weight anymore, I didn't want to think about the truth anymore, but it was inevitable. I had to call my own bluff; I wasn't going to leave the planet, and I didn't want to leave the planet. I have my amazing children and I want to see them go through this life in the best way possible. So, I had to face what I turned my back on so many years ago. I didn't realize the shame I was carrying from that moment that kept me from turning around, then my whole childhood and life flashed before my eyes. Every single major event in my life came flooding to me like a puzzle piece connecting to one other. It brought me so much clarity and insight. I remember the moment that I ripped my cross necklace off and threw it across the room. That moment stood out for what it was and showed me the moment in time that I had turned my back from the truth, from my true beliefs, from my true nature, from whom I truly was, and I sat with that memory for a while. The entire time I had my back turned to God, He never turned His back on me. Every time I took a step into the dark, He gave me a way out and I hadn't realized any of it, up until that point. Every time the devil tried to drag me to his gates, God was shining His light on me and shining on the door to escape.

I started crying harder, releasing the shame I was holding onto from that moment and asked God for forgiveness for being so blind and angry. I asked Him with every fibre of my body to forgive me for turning my back on Him and to help me change my ways so that I could do the things I truly needed to do. I then felt an overwhelming peace and love come over me that brought so much comfort, and the negative emotions, the sadness, the troubles of the world that I felt on my shoulders instantly stopped. It all stopped as that peace came over me. Then I heard a voice, a soothing, powerful fatherly voice and I knew it was God, and I didn't deny it. God said, "It's okay, child. You can rest in my arms, give me all the problems of the world that you hold; they are not yours but mine to bear. Now rest, you are protected, you are safe, and you are my child, a child of God." Ever since that night, my whole life changed. My cravings for anything outside of myself are gone. My cravings for alcohol and other things, for company that wasn't for me all went away. I started remembering more things, empowering things that I had forgotten about—things from my childhood and my curiosity and drawn towards Jesus. My curiosity made me search for answers about Him and truths about Him when I was young.

Somehow, I knew the truth about religions, as a child, that are just coming to light around the world now. I knew religions were not the way of Jesus or God but a way to control the people, to keep them in a state of fear. Religions were the first form of government and as you can see today some religions carry with them very nefarious agendas, which are not God's. Christianity was formed because of Jesus and is a beautiful religion when understood properly, but Jesus was not a Christian, He was thought to be agnostic, a free thinker, and is the Son of God. Jesus is a teacher and a healer, and He went on a mission to bring the love of God and God's words to the ears of anyone who would listen to the truth. Jesus is a free thinker, and He is the Son of God! He does not condemn, He does not judge, and He did not lie when He told the world who he was!. That's why the blind, weak and corrupted souls of the Roman Catholics so brutally tortured and nailed Him to the cross because their power came from producing fear in others and taking their power away from them through fear and submission! Meanwhile Jesus' power came from love, compassion, and understanding rooted in His spiritual nature with his Father! The second coming of Christ is here. The shadows behind the curtains are being revealed, and that is because Jesus' light is here, finally exposing all the lies for us to see, reaching the deepest corners, exposing under every rock, and all will be revealed.

"Indeed, all who desire to live a godly life in Christ Jesus will be persecuted, while evil people and imposters will go on from bad to worse, deceiving and being deceived. But as for you, continue in what you have learned and have firmly believed, knowing from whom you learned it and how from childhood you have been acquainted with the sacred writings, which are able to make you wise for salvation through faith in Christ Jesus. All scripture is breathed out by God and profitable for teaching, for reproof, for correction, and for training in righteousness, that the man of God may be complete, equipped for every good work." 2 Timothy 3:12-17 ESV

Chapter 13:
The Path

Walk with me awhile, past all the fire and the flames.
Escape this burning hell with me. Escape the sorrow and
the shame.
To feel the earth, to see the water, the air is clearing us our way . . .
Please walk with me awhile. Don't leave and go astray.
The fire burns near both of us, not too far away.
It pulls us in with heated force, as the flames dance in the night.
Although it lights its path for us, it's calling us to a fight!
A fight to lose our breath, leave us clouded, leave us maimed.
The ugly scars it'll leave us both, will just remind us of the pain.
So, walk with me awhile, stay on this path with me.
Stay far enough from the flames, until we are set free.

By: Chantel Rose

All of these moments that occurred through my life led me back to what was written in the bible. It is my belief that the bible is a sacred guidebook for us to use, to guide us through our times down here on Earth, to help us remember to seek God when we feel powerless. It is not meant to be used on innocent people who do not know better yet, to judge, condemn, or control them through fear and manipulation of the words within that book. Although many greedy, lustful and power hungry people have gotten away with hypocrisies and twist of the words in the bible, God always finds ways to serve justice righteously, and we must have patience in His vengeance.

The bible is meant to help us find the strength within us, in our faith in God to deliver us from all the evil that runs rampant on this Earth. It was never meant to be used to control, or indoctrinate, or create fear, which make people do horrendous things in the name of God. The bible was meant to teach, inspire, and give hope and strength to those succumbing to the vile thoughts that run through their heads, that usually end up leading them to hurting themselves and others. I know this because I've lived this.

There is a spiritual war going on, and this war is for our souls. Ask yourself why you are constantly battling yourself or numbing yourself or distracting yourself any way you can. To avoid seeking truth? To avoid being honest with yourself? Can you feel the spiritual war within yourself? Can you feel the back and forth tugging at you?

There is an Indigenous story that can be traced back to the Cherokee people that I like to tell my children. I ask them to ask themselves which wolf they're feeding into because you can feed the good wolf, or you can feed the bad wolf. The story goes something like this: A grandfather was explaining to his grandson that there were two wolves that lived within him. Those two wolves were battling each other for power over him. So, the grandson asks, "Well, which one wins?" and the grandfather replies, "Whichever wolf you choose to feed is the one that wins." The Indigenous Peoples of this world understand the spiritual world so beautifully and describe it with such wonderful stories and creative metaphors. What happened to them based off religious indoctrination was not what God had wanted. The words of the bible were twisted and misused to lead cultures to almost extinction. Cultures with a great connection to the spirit. It wasn't the savage these Catholic priests and nuns wanted to get rid of in the Indigenous Peoples, but it was their spirit. What happened to Indigenous Peoples worldwide was the work of the devil in disguise of humans, of priests and nuns thinking they were doing God's work within an indoctrinating controlling and bloodthirsty religion.

I am bringing this forward in my last chapter because of my Metis background. My DNA holds many memories within it and my Indigenous/European mixed background holds a lot of trauma within my ancestral line that I can feel. That I can feel getting ready to be cleansed fully through knowing ones worth and self-love in such a way that I will hold peace with loving power in my heart even after all the traumatic events that surrounded me in this lifetime and the lifetimes before. When you learn to connect to your spiritual essence you remember who you really are.

The Indigenous Peoples already knew the spirit of the land, mother nature, the goodness of what the land gave them to survive, and the abundance of their environment. They were trusting; they spoke to Spirit regularly asking for guidance, they were nurturers of their environment, and not wasteful of anything. They took care of the land, and the land took care of them. They received things with good blessings and love in their hearts, but did they exactly know God, did they exactly know Jesus? No, they did not. The Indigenous only knew their own spiritual essence that they could feel surrounding them and taking care of them, but they didn't call it what those priests and nuns called it, and that was where the trouble arose for them.

Religious doctrines thought it was their right to go around the world spreading the word of God through their misinterpreted perspectives and that anything or anyone that didn't line up to their ways were considered savages. THIS WAS NOT TRUE; these religions twisted the word of God in such a way to justify the rape and pillage and genocide of people, of cultures. When there is raping, and genocide, and executions of innocent blood, that is not God, that is the devil at work twisting you up with his lies! The atrocities brought to indigenous people because of religious indoctrination was the work of the devil. Governments and religions, in a team effort, built residential schools to beat the "savage",spirit, out of the indigenous people. Indigenous people still to this day you can see their hope and inspiration from overcoming all the atrocities against them. The spirit is strong within Indigenous cultures, why do you think the devil wants to get rid of them. With love and trust still in the hearts of Indigenous people, even from the major trauma imposed on them, they are coming back to life now. They are thriving and spreading their good strong spirit across the world again. Indigenous people did not give up, they did not give in, and you can see in the world today the generational trauma is starting to heal within the different Indigenous cultures. With their humor, beauty, and strong spirit they have taken over social media platforms and are paving a way of light and strength for future generations.

The trusting, loving, non-judgmental, giving, nurturing, and natural healing ways of the indigenous people are closer to the path that Jesus walked then what these religious leaders, popes, and priests walked and still pretend to walk. The indigenous people were walking a path closer to Jesus' before they even knew who He was. A lot of the religions, especially catholic, pretend to walk a Godly path, but they don't and I'm not afraid to speak out about it anymore. You can see in the people, in place at the Vatican, how dark they really are, how many sickening secrets they hold and how they do not walk the path of righteousness, they do not walk the path of Godliness, and how they hoard the riches of the world like the greedy blood thirsty creatures that they are. But like I said before, the light is here, and it is bright, and it is blinding, and it will start to burn those who CHOOSE to walk with the devil. Not the ones who accidently got lost in his lies and are searching for a way out, but those who knew and still chose to walk with the devil, for power over the people, and for greed.

I am talking about those that did the devil's work, those that raped, tortured, and almost killed an entire culture. By now I hope you understand why the title is the way it is. Those unholy people had no Holy Spirit within them, they were just covered in the devil's filthy lies, but the time for justice is upon them. It is finally time for the Indigenous cultures of the world to rise once again in their full glory and those that betrayed their trust and tried to take their spirit away, will be thrown into the lake of fire for eternity. Those that walk with the devil and do the devils work will be thrown into the pits of hell. God gave them free will. God gave them the ability to discern between truth and lies, between good and evil. God gave them the bible and his prophets for guidance and for clarity. God gave those, now unholy people, HIS

SON, JESUS, FOR REDEMPTION, FOR THE CLEANSING OF SIN, AND THOSE PEOPLE SPIT IN GOD'S FACE. So now the unholy people of this world shall reap what they've sown.

When I wrote earlier that there is a spiritual warfare going on for your soul, I meant it. Satan wants your soul for his own selfish and vile reasons. He doesn't care about you he just wants to stack up the bodies as trophies to say, SEE, SEE WHO I HAVE GOTTEN TO SIN, TO TURN AWAY FROM YOU, GOD! God will do everything in his power to hold on to you, to show you signs, to show you reason, but he did give you free will, free will to choose, free will to discern between what's good and what's evil and if you let go of his Right hand willingly, there's not much more He can do. God will sit and pray for you to overcome the temptation and He waits with his arms wide open, ready to embrace you as His child once again. Although you haven't been able to see Him in the flesh, like you see the physical things around you, He prays for your strong faith in Him, in the unseen. You do not need the bible, or a church, to hear God, to pray to God, or to seek God's words, but it is a good start in practicing who to listen for when you are just recognizing and remembering, who you truly are. Which is a child of God.

For those who think hell is not real, why wouldn't it be? It's been the longest story running since the dawn of time. That's why I used that old Cherokee story in the beginning of this chapter because it resonated with me to my core because I can feel the spiritual warfare going on inside of me. I have felt it since I was a child but had no clue until now what was going on. I can feel the shift in energy and have learned which wolf to feed depending on my situation. Sometimes I feel I have to match fire to fire because some beings down here don't know love at all or their love was lost long ago, but fear, fear makes them respond. When you're in a dangerous situation sometimes fear is the only thing you can use against someone who is on their way to harm you. It is a double edged sword good vs evil but with that knowledge you need to be aware of which wolf you are feeding and why. There is balance in life and when the scales are tipped that's when chaos ensues, that's why we must be mindful of the environment we are helping to create.

What are intentions in this lifetime? To create a loving environment or a hateful one?

It is my belief that we are not the creators of our reality BUT the CO-CREATORS with God. He blesses us with His grace and fulfills wishes we ask Him, if it is for your best interests and His will. He didn't control Lucifer and gave Lucifer his wish. Which was to have his own Kingdom like God has, but Lucifer was also jealous of God's creation of humanity, God's love of humans, of His children. There is a righteous jealousy and a self-righteous jealousy, Lucifer no longer felt like God's eyes were mostly on him anymore with the creation of humans. So, Lucifer's self-righteous jealousy and lust, for the omnipotent power that God has, created a monster within him and he was able to convince other angels to fall with him in sin. Lucifer who was once the most beautiful angel, the morning star, is now a monster. That monster, who is known as the devil, then created the split between him and God. God is all loving and righteous and He has given us all Free Will. So, rather than destroying Lucifer, he watched him fashion his own kingdom, but it is in complete opposite of what God is and so there is hell. By no means is the devil more powerful than God just because he has his own kingdom, but he can manipulate humanity and take souls for his collection. There has to be balance. How could we know the good without the bad? It all serves it's purpose.

The path to God's house, to Heaven, is narrow and just like you wouldn't allow just anyone into your home, what makes you think God would? He may be all powerful and loving but He is also righteous and justified in His judgments. God is cheering you on to overcome such sinful things and He knows your past does not define you. The bad things you may have done do not define you, as long as you seek forgiveness, seek the truth of your sin, and most importanty seek God for guidance. When you ask for these things, then God knows your heart is of good intention and you intentionally want to change to be a better person. He then knows you want to overcome all these obstacles placed on your path that have led you astray and wants you to come to Him to fill your cup up with His abundance, His love, His protection, and His grace. By no means does it mean to not have fun and enjoy your life, for great joy is found close to God, trust me, the purity of it all is brilliant.

The devil has done quite the job convincing people otherwise and when the devil is done with you, your smiles will fade as the fun ends. You'll be sucked into a cycle of pain, become a trophy on his burning wall, and fade away into darkness. No one knows when another opportunity to redeem yourself will become available, so choose wisely. God gave us free will to see what lay deep in our hearts, deep in our souls, and wants you to practice discerning between good and evil, and walk the path that Jesus would have wanted you to walk. Not what any religions say but what Jesus taught and would have wanted you to do. For the path you walk will either bring you back into God's loving embrace or into the pits of hell. I've been on both paths, so that's why I am telling you this. When I came back to God, I received all this information to write this book, to put it together in such a way in hopes you would remember the truth of it all.

Prior to writing this book and remembering who I truly am, I always had a feeling in my heart that at some point, the deceiptful fun had to come to an end. My life has been a myriad of different experiences and I feel like I have lived several lifetimes within this one. I had many great learning experiences while travelling around the world and understanding the darker sides of life while maintaining a lighter way of being. My journey to discovering is not over and I have many things to sift and sort through still. To learn and unlearn. What I do know is I have found peace in knowing that there is more to life than what we see around us. You can feel the power within the still and silent moments you give yourself. Sometimes just being and not doing anything can lead you to many more things than you can imagine. Give yourself the opportunity to bask in silent reflection of your being and pull forth the power within you to see clearly. The peace you gain and the calming of the storm within is a divine feeling. When I say the world is not what you think it is, please seek the truth of it. Find your faith in the unseen, rise above like a phoenix through the fire, and be reborn through the Son of God and back into God's loving arms. I love you and God bless.

> "Jesus said to him, 'I am the way, and the truth, and the life. No one comes to the Father except through me.'" John 14:6 ESV

CPSIA information can be obtained
at www.ICGtesting.com
Printed in the USA
LVHW100055161121
703452LV00013B/640/J